D1403471

LOST LANDSCAPES

LOST LANDSCAPES

In Search of Isaac Bashevis Singer and the Jews of Poland

AGATA TUSZYŃSKA

Translated from Polish by Madeline G. Levine

WILLIAM MORROW AND COMPANY, INC. NEW YORK

UNIVERSITY OF TOLEDO LIBRARIES

Copyright © 1998 by Agata Tuszyńska

Translation copyright © 1998 by Madeline G. Levine

Grateful acknowledgment is made for permission to reprint the following:

A fragment of "Jan Mazurek's Chronicle." Permission granted by the Regional Museum of Tomaszów Lubelski, Poland.

By permission of Farrar, Straus & Giroux, Inc.:
Excerpt from "The Unseen," translated by Norbert Gutterman and Elaine Gottlieb, from *The Collected Stories* by Isaac Bashevis Singer. Copyright © 1982 by Isaac Bashevis Singer. Excerpts from *The Family Moskat* by Isaac Bashevis Singer, translated by A. H. Gross. Translation copyright © 1950 by Alfred A. Knopf, and copyright © renewed 1977 by Isaac Bashevis Singer. Excerpt from *Love and Exile* by Isaac Bashevis Singer. Copyright © 1984 by Isaac Bashevis Singer. Excerpt from *Scum* by Isaac Bashevis Singer, translated by Rosaline Dukalsky Schwartz. Translation copyright © 1991 by Isaac Bashevis Singer.

All rights reserved. No part of this book may be reproduced or utilized in any form or by any means, electronic or mechanical, including photocopying, recording, or by any information storage or retrieval system, without permission in writing from the Publisher. Inquiries should be addressed to Permissions Department, William Morrow and Company, Inc., 1350 Avenue of the Americas, New York, N.Y. 10019.

It is the policy of William Morrow and Company, Inc., and its imprints and affiliates, recognizing the importance of preserving what has been written, to print the books we publish on acid-free paper, and we exert our best efforts to that end.

Library of Congress Cataloging-in-Publication Data

Tuszyńska, Agata.
    [Singer. English]
    Lost landscapes : in search of Isaac Bashevis Singer and the Jews of Poland / Agata Tuszyńska ; translated from Polish by Madeline G. Levine.
      p. cm.
    ISBN 0-688-12214-0
    1. Singer, Isaac Bashevis, 1904–1991. 2. Authors, Yiddish—United States—Biography. 3. Jews—Poland—Social life and customs.
    I. Title.
    PJ5129.S49Z9513 1998
    839'.133—dc21
    [B]
                                            97-21245
                                             CIP

Printed in the United States of America

First Edition

1 2 3 4 5 6 7 8 9 10

BOOK DESIGN BY LEAH S. CARLSON

PJ
5129
.S49Z9513
1998

⅝| ACKNOWLEDGMENTS |⅝

This book was shaped by other people's memories, and I am grateful to all those who agreed to deposit with me fragments of their personal histories. Without their intensely private, often painful memories, my landscapes would have remained barren, unpopulated, and hollow. I thank all those witnesses to the past, both Polish and Jewish, whose voices may be found on the pages of this book.

I had the good fortune to benefit from the help and advice of my teachers and friends. In the United States: the late Professor Lucjan Dobroszycki of YIVO, Professors Rachmiel Peltz of Columbia University and David Roskies of the Jewish Theological Seminary, attorney Ludwik Seidenman, and Larry Mayer; in Poland: the late Andrzej Drawicz, Ludwik B. Grzeniewski, Michael Sobelman, and the late poet Wiktor Woroszylski.

I appreciate the generosity of the Fulbright Foundation in Washington, D.C., which awarded me a research fellowship, and the financial assistance of the Kosciuszko Foundation in New York and the American Jewish Archives in Cincinnati.

My special thanks go to Henry Dasko, my most faithful companion during the several years of my work on this book.

CONTENTS

PART ONE

Singer

I was late for his death.

Isaac Bashevis Singer died on July 24, 1991, in Florida. He was eighty-seven years old.

For several years he had been suffering from an illness that causes loss of memory. How could that be? After all, he had lived by memory, been nourished by it—by his own memory and the memories of other people. When it was gone, he left this world. He died peacefully, staring up at the ceiling. In silence.

Isaac Bashevis Singer was my first guide within the world of Polish Jewry. Before I was able to understand the word "Jew," the Jews had ceased to exist as a community. The reality that Singer described was as distant and inaccessible for me as the era of the pharaohs or ancient Romans, yet, instinctively, it was closer. I sensed, more than recognized, its traces around me, in the ruins of synagogues and shattered symbols.

I did not know of Singer's existence until that moment in 1978 when he received the Nobel Prize in Literature. I also knew nothing before that time about the world whose chronicler he was.

I didn't know any Jews, or at least I thought I didn't. No one had taught me their history or customs. Or pointed out how deeply rooted they were in this land that was mine. No one made me aware of the foundations of the centuries-long Polish-Jewish heritage.

Singer's books, read one after another, opened up for me that hitherto closed universe. Even more important, they began filling out the missing pages of my own fate.

The internalized space of my childhood memories was Kazimierz on the Vistula, a small city in the Lublin region, about seventy-five miles from Warsaw. I spent every summer vacation there. All my initial impressions are from Kazimierz. On the riverbank or in the ravines, in the marketplace with its well, not far from a monastery or parish church, or on the Mount of Three Crosses.

I watched children's films in a movie theater that was unlike any other. It was small, rather squat, with a high vaulted ceiling and a purposeless little balcony. The hill at Czerniawy was our favorite spot for playing, where for years we dug in the earth with unfailing patience. We unearthed moss-covered stones, overgrown with time and sadness. We uncovered fragments of inscriptions in an unknown language, crippled reliefs of lions, or, occasionally, sketches of clasped hands, their fingers intertwined. The hunchbacked stones attracted us with their homeless secret.

Kazimierz saw itself depicted on many canvases. In the marketplace, the arcades, we looked it over in innumerable mirrors. In oils and watercolors, pencil and charcoal, from a bird's-eye view and in the smallest detail of holidays and market days. The images were populated with figures in black suits, hats with fox fur brims, cloth caps. In vain I looked for them among the local inhabitants.

I began to recognize them at last in the Gimpels, Aarons, Szyjas, and Shmuls on the pages of Singer's prose. Soon not only their dress but also the ritual of their lives became a matter of course for me. Singer helped me reconstruct my shattered world. Wasn't it mine? Shouldn't it have been mine? After all, in story after story I recognized the geography of Polish cities and localities. All this had taken place here, in Kazimierz on the Vistula. Moreover, it had happened recently, within the memory of living witnesses. Here too, as in countless Polish towns, Jews had lived, engaged in trade, prayed, and died. For so many years, unconsciously, I had connected with the places of their daily life: the market in the square, the little stores and workshops, the house of prayer and the house of death.

My movie theater—severe, cold, devoid, to be sure, of the particular melody of prayerful voices, but obviously wiser than any ordinary movie house—was a Jewish synagogue. The hilltop at Czerniawy, overgrown with trees, grass, and nettles, it turned out was the final resting place of the Kazimierz Jews in the time when they were still dying peaceful deaths.

I wanted to return them to the places they belonged to, to give back their home to the orphaned, even if only on paper. To open up the scar and allow them to return home.

Singer, the only Nobel laureate of Yiddish literature and the homeless Yiddish language, the author of "Gimpel the Fool," *The Family Moskat*, and *The Magician of Lublin*, came from a Jewish family that had lived beside the Vistula River for six hundred years. We can assume that were it not for the war and Hitler's madness, it would have been possible to visit his grave in the Jewish cemetery on Gęsia Street in Warsaw, not far from the places where he spent his childhood and youth. That he wound up across the ocean and his literary maturation occurred in America is a matter of historical accident.

Had he remained in Poland and had he survived, his fate—as a creative writer too—would certainly have been different. Would firsthand experience of annihilation have allowed him to paint with equal power his landscapes of memory of a world destroyed? Or were his breadth, his chronicler's perseverance and zeal, the result of his having abandoned that world? Deprived of his familiar, life-giving soil, he saved himself through his memories. He allowed everything that he once knew to take up residence inside him: all those figures and seasons of the Jewish canvas, which he reconstructed repeatedly, indefatigably, over many years. Narrating the history of the Polish Jews, their fervor and their everyday existence, made him into the legendary zaddik of twentieth-century Jewish literature.

He lived in New York longer than he lived in Poland, but he never really made the move to America. He wore the past like an overcoat, whatever the season. His permanent address remained in Poland. That was where he was born, where he learned about the world, where he lived in one tenement house after another, where Jewishness was the air people breathed. His literary fate was inscribed in a specific geographical and spiritual space.

Before World War II three million Jews lived in Poland; Warsaw's Jewish population was second only to New York City's. Barely a few thousand remain. Today no letter will reach a Radzymin or Biłgoraj rabbi. There are no rabbis. There are no Jewish tailors or watchmakers. Their homes no longer exist. Searching for traces of their presence in Poland—in the land where they lived for more than seven hundred years—is, as the poet Jerzy Ficowski has written, like deciphering ashes.

I was late for his world. For cholent and challah, for the Sabbath holy day, and for faith in the infallibility of the Torah.

He left Warsaw relatively recently, in 1935. Many people can remember those days. They remember how much a liter of vodka cost and that the price of a streetcar ticket had been reduced to twenty groschen; they remember the novelty of the stock exchange and aberrations in the weather. No one remembers the Singer brothers, both of them talented writers, or their family. It is almost as if the testimony of their books were the only proof that they really existed.

Had they been Poles, a search for their documents and for witnesses would never have created so many difficulties. The Polish writers who frequented the Warsaw literary café, the Ziemiańska, left behind an infinite number of portraits in gossip and in memoirs. The Jewish writers who sat at similar café tables at No. 13 Tłomackie Street—which was not so far away after all—do not exist in either the consciousness or the memory of Polish intellectuals.

Language was the barrier that delineated spheres of influence. Their worlds were as distant from each other as Jewish Nalewki Street and Polish Marszałkowska, even though people of all religious denominations used to go to the synagogue on Tłomackie Street to hear its famous cantors. Jewish Poland, with its *peyes* (side curls) and long black gaberdines, only rarely came into contact with Polish Poland, with its processions on Corpus Christi Day and its boxes at the Grand Theater. And although Singer could certainly speak Polish, it was not his language, the language in which he expressed his feelings, or the language of his thoughts.

On Krochmalna Street, where Singer lived, the only Gentiles were watchmen and letter carriers. How can I find the maids who worked in the houses on Leszno and Gęsia streets where he rented cheap rooms? In little towns near Warsaw and

Lublin old men who resemble the demons in his stories still shuffle about near the marketplace. They limp, their faces ravaged, their voices hoarse from drink, and for want of anything better to do they summon the spirits of the past. These are my guides among the remnants of the graves, the remnants of the synagogues, the remnants of the traces. Among the traces of the traces of their lives and final roads. The Jews who might have remembered perished. Those who did survive emigrated. And over there too they are dying out. There are fewer and fewer of them. The last ones.

I was too late, and so this story will be sewn, braided, knotted together from the memories of others, from scraps, crumbs, remnants. From old photographs, fragments of surviving letters, shoestrings from the stockpiles at Auschwitz. I was too late; therefore, I shall describe the shapes of absence, memory lapses.

His birth certificate does not exist. Was it consumed by flames during the last war along with so many other documents? And so many volumes of the holy books, which, under normal conditions, Jews would have disposed of by burial? How insignificant this is in relation to the deaths of people, thousands, millions of people, for whom communal black books have replaced ordinary notations in registries of births, marriages, deaths. Perhaps the birth certificate of Isaac Bashevis, the future Nobel laureate, was destroyed during the First World War? In Leoncin, where he was born, with the records of the Jewish congregation in Zakroczym, or maybe in Radzymin, where he seems to have been registered, although he was already three years old at the time?

But it is not just this one document that is missing.

I searched in town halls, where these sorts of documents are usually preserved for a hundred years, but nothing could be found. Occasionally I would stumble accidentally upon a congregation registry, but neither the locality nor the dates were a match. A few such registries had survived; they were found in the ruins, extricated from rubbish heaps, dug up from under the earth. Sometimes people brought papers they were unable to decipher to teachers or to a museum. Even photographs turned up on occasion. More often the papers were used as kindling. In Biłgoraj after the war herring was sold wrapped in pages from the Wilno Torah. In Piaski, also in the Lublin district, somebody rescued about a dozen volumes from the registry of the Jewish congregation, the *gmina*.

To find documents that go back more than one hundred years, one is supposed to look in local archives. But Poland's archives were destroyed or abducted—and not just during the last war, so there is not much one can find there. This is true not only in relation to Jewish history. The materials are haphazard, and often there are more empty spaces than there are items on the shelves and in the catalogs.

Singer's father traced his family back to the famed Baal Shem Tov, the founder of Hasidism. His genealogical tree reached back through Sabbatai Kohen, Rabbi Moses Isserles, and Rashi, all the way to King David. In the first half of the twentieth century they lived in the hamlet of Leoncin, in the little towns of Biłgoraj and Radzymin, and, of course, in Warsaw. I sent letters to every archive in the Lublin district. Is it possible that not a single document survived?

The street directory of Warsaw residents for the year 1909–1910 lists a Pinchas Singer, Isaac Bashevis's father, on Krochmalna Street, plus twenty-two other Singers. Most of them are merchants, four on Twarda Street and the others on Nalewki, Miła, and Śliska. There is also a writer on Ciepła Street and a musician on Krucza. Singer's father doesn't appear even once in the telephone directory. Aside from Singer sewing machines, which had warehouses and dealers in several districts of the city, the only Singers who had telephones were senior paramedics and physicians.

All the buildings on that stretch of Krochmalna Street where he lived were destroyed during the bombings at the beginning of the last war. Whatever remained standing was demolished during the fighting in the Warsaw Uprising of 1944. After the war the area was leveled and the ground was covered over with the foundations for a new residential district, which occupies almost the entire area of the old Jewish quarter. It is a vast, utterly impersonal expanse; you would search in vain for any traces of the past there. History has been erased from this space; old landscapes have been nullified. Memory has been gagged. Could that be the reason why someone struggled for so many years to prevent the destruction of the remaining fragments of the ghetto wall between Sienna and Złota streets? People didn't understand what the point was; after all, the monument to the Heroes of the Ghetto was nearby, and in 1988 a symbolic wall, a monument to Umschlagplatz—the assembly point for the Jews who were to be deported from Warsaw—was erected on Stawki Street. From the upper stories of the tall buildings on what used to be Gęsia Street one can see the Jewish cemetery.

There are no buildings, no tenements, no houses, yet once they were someone's property. The only document I was able to find was the plat for the buildings at No. 10 and No. 12 Krochmalna Street, where the Singer family lived between 1908 and 1917.

They had a hard time paying the monthly rent of twenty-four rubles for an apartment with a front-facing balcony. A new apartment, with gas lighting and an indoor toilet, would have cost three rubles more. In 1914 a carpenter or a clerk would have had to work two days to earn that amount; that was how much a hundred nails or two poods (seventy-two pounds) of kerosene cost. A pound of tea cost more than four rubles.

The document found inside the "pocket"—a supplemental folder inside the Krochmalna Street real estate register—is a map of the whole property, written in Russian, as were all official documents after the January 1863 uprising. Without Singer, the plat that lies before me would be only an architectural document. In *Love and Exile*, Isaac Bashevis Singer remembered that entire "city" in detail, with its three enormous, well-like courtyards. Ryfka, with her tambourine and a parrot with a broken beak on her shoulder, wandered through them, as did old-clothes dealers and street magicians who swallowed fire or walked on rolling barrels. Laundry was hung out to dry on wooden balconies. Two Hasidic study houses—for the Radzymin and the Minsk Hasidim—were there, as was a synagogue for the opponents of Hasidism and a pen in which cows were kept chained to the wall year-round. The bakery was directly across from their apartment. In the cellars the Mirowski Market stallkeepers stored fruit or pickled eggs in lime. Singer remembered that his home "swarmed with Torah, prayer, commerce and toil."

The list of the owners of both properties is a long one, and the enumeration of their financial obligations and maneuvers even longer and more detailed. But nowhere is there any mention of Rabbi Singer, the father. He was never late with the rent; he never borrowed; he never made any trouble. Nowhere is there evidence of his activities: resolving disputes, granting divorces, performing marriages. Not a trace of the life of the tenants. No complaints about the communal privy in the courtyard, the scourge of Isaac Bashevis's childhood. About the rats and mice that ran around underfoot. About the filth in the stairwell, which the children preferred over the courtyard privy and which some of the women used as a garbage chute.

Not a word about the watchman who wasn't particularly conscientious about performing his job of lighting the lamps in the stairwells. So, did a small red-haired boy, who was terrified of demons and apparitions, really live there? And what became of the smell of that place, the smell of frying oil, rotten fruit, and smoke?

Both houses on Krochmalna Street were turned over to the Polish state treasury in April 1965. Fifteen years earlier Singer had written *The Family Moskat*, in which he resurrected demolished Warsaw for the first time. *Shosha*, in which he denies the death of that world, came into being thirteen years later.

In one of his stories he describes a young man who is wandering through the ruins of Warsaw like the prophet Jeremiah. He keeps on digging up the earth with his spade. When asked what he is looking for, he replies: "Myself."

Singer did not want to return to Poland. He did not want to return to a cemetery. He had the ground beneath his feet only within his memory.

I could not find him anywhere.

Months went by before a letter arrived in a gray envelope bearing the seal of the city archives of Zamość, a town near Lublin.

"We hereby inform you," it said, "that in the Biłgoraj Marriage Bureau registry for citizens of the Mosaic faith, volume 14, we have located under entry number 10 from 1889 a record of the marriage of the parents of Isaac Bashevis Singer. . . ."

⅃| THE BEGINNING |Ɛ

The Zamość record is the only documentary reference to Isaac Bashevis Singer's family I was able to trace in Poland. Dated 1889, the marriage record of Singer's parents begins:

> In the city of Biłgoraj, the second (fourteenth) day of June, 1889, at six in the evening, Jankiel Gudes, sixty-six years old, and Lina Fajner, fifty years old, both rabbis resident in the city of Biłgoraj, presented themselves and testified that on this day a religious marriage contract was concluded between Mendel Pinchas Singer, twenty-one years old, a bachelor still living with his parents, born in the city of Tomaszów, Lublin Province, son of Szmul and Tema (née Szejner) Singer, residents of the city of Tomaszów, and Miss Szeva Zylberman, eighteen years old, still living with her parents, born in the town of P[illegible] in Volhynia Province, daughter of Jakub Mordechai and his wife Chana (née Danziger) Zylberman, residents of the city of Biłgoraj. . . .

The marriage was preceded by three formal announcements. The religious ritual of marriage was performed by the bride's father, Jakub Mordechai Zylberman, the Biłgoraj district rabbi.

The document was written in Cyrillic.

The year was 5649 according to the Jewish calendar. Biłgoraj, the third-largest city in the Lublin district, under Russian administration for several decades by then, had unpaved streets, wooden houses roofed with shingles, and no sewers. Since 1880 thirteen regiments of Don Cossacks had been stationed there. Orthodox Jews accounted for 40 percent of the population. They controlled all the trade and the taverns.

Sheva (Batsheva) Zylberman bore Rabbi Pinchas Singer four children. Two came into the world in Biłgoraj: a daughter, Hindele Esther, in 1891, and a son, Israel Joshua, two years later. Both became writers, just like their brother, the Nobel laureate. Isaac Bashevis Singer was born in 1904 in Leoncin, near Warsaw, and so was his younger brother, Moshe, in 1906. Their father had obtained an unofficial junior rabbinical post there. According to the policies in effect in the partitioned Polish lands under Russian rule, the so-called Vistula Lands, the father's inability to speak Russian condemned him to hold only minor positions. Such posts came Pinchas Singer's way in Leoncin, in Radzymin, and then on Krochmalna Street in Warsaw.

When the Singers left Biłgoraj at the turn of the century, thirty-five hundred Jews lived there. Today there is not a single one. Leoncin and Radzymin were almost 100 percent Jewish. Before the war Warsaw's Krochmalna Street was a kingdom of the Jewish poor. No one speaks Yiddish today in any of those places.

The Singers came to Leoncin from Biłgoraj around 1897 and stayed ten years. A chronicle of their Leoncin period was left by Isaac's brother Joshua, who was eleven years older. In his memoir *Of a World That Is No More*, he calls Leoncin a village. About forty families lived there, or close to two hundred people. He remembers the single two-story house, decorated with balconies, the sandy streets, the signs above the cloth and grocery stores, the Puss in Boots figurine in the window of the tobacco shop. He looked at the world through shards of colored glass that he and his friends collected on the grounds of the only factory in Leoncin, a kvass brewery. In Leoncin there were two stores that belonged to Gentiles: In one, pork was sold, and in the other, beer and vodka.

The Leoncin rabbi's home was like a study house. In the guest room the Ark rested upon Torah scrolls. Two carved, gilded lions held the tablets of Moses in their mouths. God seemed to control this place in which everything might prove to be a sin. The brothers remember their father bowed over his lectern, studying the great books and constantly writing something in the margins. The youngsters had no toys; they played with tomes of the holy books, with a broken pen, an empty ink bottle, or pieces of paper.

Images of several towns live in his childhood memory: Leoncin on the Vistula, even though they moved away when he was not quite three years old; Radzymin, where his father became a yeshiva teacher in 1907. From there he remembers a fire in the rabbi's courtyard and the commotion that accompanied it, like the end of the world. A year later the Singer family moved to Warsaw, to Krochmalna Street. That was where he grew up.

Warsaw's Krochmalna Street, an ancient cart track, was transformed into a street in the second half of the seventeenth century. Over the next hundred years it was built up with four-story buildings and private residences, mainly of wood, among orchards and gardens, and was called Lawendowa Street. It had four breweries, two distilleries, and a starchworks. At the end of the eighteenth century it was given the name Krochmalna, which means Starch Street. At that time too one section was paved. At the end of the nineteenth century many tenement houses were built there; they were inhabited for the most part by Jews.

From 1940 to 1942 Krochmalna Street lay within the boundaries of the so-called Little Ghetto. In 1944 the buildings along the street were destroyed, with the exception of a few houses on Żelazna and between Towarowa and Karolkowa streets. After the war a plaque was placed at No. 92 in honor of Janusz Korczak, who had served as director of the Jewish Orphans' Home since 1912. After 1969 Krochmalna Street was built up with the large buildings of a municipal housing project.

From 1908 the Singer family lived on Krochmalna Street—for six years as an intact family. In 1914 the two oldest siblings,

Hindele Esther and Israel Joshua, moved out, and in 1917 the two youngest, Isaac and Moshe, left with their mother for Biłgoraj, fleeing the hunger in German-occupied Warsaw. Many unusual things happened in No. 12 Krochmalna Street, a house full of holiness, but inhabited too by hobgoblins, demons, dybbuks, and devils. Family legend affirms that Rabbi Singer believed in them as firmly as he denied the existence of electricity.

Rabbi Singer's study was like a wailing wall for the poor Jews of Krochmalna Street. For the future author of *Shosha*, their confessions and stories were a kind of academy where he studied human behavior and passions. From childhood on, he was surrounded by tales of people's madness, cruelty, and love.

On Krochmalna Street he read the Old Testament for the first time and immediately after it *The Adventures of Sherlock Holmes* in a Yiddish translation and Dostoevsky's *Crime and Punishment*. Through his brother Israel Joshua, he learned of the existence of Archimedes, Copernicus, Newton, and Descartes. He came into contact with forbidden thought. Yet on Krochmalna Street sorrow because of the destruction of the Temple always seemed more immediate than current events.

Isaac was eleven when Isaac Peretz died, the sole classic writer of modern Jewish literature who had Polish ties. A year later Sholem Aleichem passed away, and right after him, Mendele Mocher Sforim. The books of these writers were just as much an abomination in his father's eyes as the novels of Gentile writers. For the Singers' father, absorbed in religious contemplation, the world was *treyf* (not kosher).

The eldest son, Israel Joshua, was the first to try to liberate himself from religious strictures. He grew more and more rebellious toward Orthodox tradition. He attempted to show his father his own vision of the world, using names like Newton, Copernicus, Spinoza. He talked about Zionism and revolution, about the necessity of coming to terms with the new reality. His younger brother listened to these discussions, seeking within himself confirmation of both sides. He was attracted by Joshua's ideas, but they didn't provide the sense of security that the parental faith offered. It would not be long before he too broke with it. Yet he would not hesitate to seek support in religion when everything else failed. His Krochmalna Street inheritance nurtured him for years.

Israel Joshua soon cut his *peyess* and cast aside his gaberdine. He moved into an atelier with young artists who smoked on the Sabbath, drank milk with their meat, and painted naked women. He began to think seriously about a literary career. His younger brother soon followed in his footsteps.

There are two known photographs of the two of them together. In one, a young man with a thin face stands next to a teenage Hasid dressed in a black cap with a narrow brim, his *peyess* tucked behind his ears. Both look straight ahead, the first with a cold, penetrating gaze; the second as if under a spell, with rapturous incredulity. The first is issuing a challenge to the world. The second displays childlike fascination.

The next photograph, taken probably ten years later, accentuates these traits. And although both men now have short hair and wear similar dark suits and ties, the younger is again overwhelmed by the figure of the older. Joshua sits in the pose of a conqueror, with his hands crossed on his knees. Isaac's gaze, from behind dark-framed glasses, is fleeing somewhere off to the side. His hands are placed shyly on his knees. He seems to be his brother's shadow.

Isaac called Warsaw the city of his dreams and hopes. He came there a second time in mid-1923 to take a job as proofreader at the Yiddish literary weekly *Literarishe Bleter*, which his brother, then the paper's editor, had arranged for him. It was he who gave him his first literary advice and pointers.

Israel Joshua's collection of short stories *Pearls* caught the attention not only of Warsaw's literary circles but also of the New York press. The editor of a Yiddish paper in New York offered him a contract as a permanent contributor, which instantly turned him into a wealthy man by Polish standards.

According to the census of September 30, 1921, there were almost three million "citizens of the Mosaic faith" in Poland—over 10 percent of the population. More than three hundred thousand of them—one third of the capital's population—lived in Warsaw.

They formed a varied community. They accounted for almost half the Warsaw bourgeoisie, the industrialists, owners of great wholesale firms, warehouses, and tenement houses. One out of two Warsaw doctors in private practice was a Jew, even more of the lawyers.

Eighty-four percent of all small-shop owners, stallkeepers, street vendors, peddlers whose goods dangled on their arms or were carried in a wooden case ("combs, ties, shoelaces our specialty") came from the Jewish poor.

The same percentage of Jews spoke and read Yiddish.

They had their own Yiddish-language schools—cheders and yeshivas—and also a large network of periodicals. In Warsaw alone several dozen journals were published, and half a dozen or so daily newspapers, weekly cultural supplements, humor magazines, women's magazines, children's magazines.

According to the *Warsaw Crime Statistics* for the years 1926–1935, Jews committed less than one third of all crimes. In the categories of homicides and crimes against "sexual morality," they account for an insignificant percentage. They figure much more prominently in swindles (forging checks, bank notes, etc.). Under "taking bribes," the number is zero, under "suborning," or giving bribes, as high as 35 percent.

By the mid-1920s the Jewish study houses were beginning to empty out. The youth were moving away from their ancient faith, discovering hope in socialism, communism, Zionism. They yearned to be free of their parents' long coats and little shops, to tear themselves away at any price from "that quagmire." Spiritual revolution was an unquestioned fact. Repelled by every type of collectivism and all dictatorships, young Singer stood on the sidelines.

He published his first text—about the Hebrew-language literary monthly *HaShiloah*—under the pseudonym Isaac Tsey in 1924. The piece appeared in *Literarishe Bleter*, the respected Yiddish weekly. At that time the best-known novels in Poland were Stefan Żeromski's *Before the Spring* and Zofia Nałkowska's *The Romance of Teresa Hennert*. Joseph Conrad and Anatole France died that year. Thomas Mann published *The Magic Mountain*. Władysław Reymont, author of *The Peasants,* received the Nobel Prize in Literature. Singer's first story in Yiddish, under the title "For Old Age," appeared one year later in the same magazine, where it won a prize in a literary competition. It was also then that he adopted a nom de plume, Bashevis (from Batsheva, his mother's name), so that he would not be confused with his older brother.

In the Writers' Club at No. 13 Tłomackie, where he spent a great deal of time, he was always referred to as Singer's brother. An aura of the distinguished writer surrounded Israel Joshua by the end of the twenties. People envied him his position and his talent.

Both brothers wrote in Yiddish, because that was the language their protagonists used. The younger brother's choice was no doubt influenced by the older brother's writings, but also by his friendship and collaboration with the distinguished Yiddish poet Aaron Zeitlin and his ties with *Literarishe Bleter*.

He published book reviews, interviews, and short stories, and he supplemented his earnings with translations from the German, including Mann's *The Magic Mountain* and prose works by Gabriele d'Annunzio, Knut Hamsun, Arnold Zweig. In order to earn more money, he also adapted popular German novels for the Yiddish afternoon papers. He was always short of money.

His frequent moves abetted his inate absentmindedness; he lost his documents and all his various identity papers. The protagonists in his prose works often inherited this trait, which makes them into a particular variation of the Jewish everyman. His dress was absentminded too: his tie askew, trousers that looked as if they could fall down at any moment, shoelaces untied. Yet women liked him. A blue-eyed, pale redhead, with flame red ears and hunched shoulders, he himself did not understand the secret of his success. Pathologically shy, he was perhaps amusing in his helplessness. He called himself an "indefatigable lover" and insisted that he "lived like a libertine," but in company he became a cheder boy.

In the summer of 1932 Israel Joshua Singer's new novel *Yoshe Kalb* appeared in installments in the *Forward* in New York and in a Polish-Jewish newspaper, *The Moment*, in Lwów. This story of Nachum, a zaddik's son from Rachmaninówka, and his criminal love for his father-in-law's young wife, is a drama of passion and sin, suffering and penance, guilt and punishment.

Their father had told both brothers this story many times. Joshua wrote it down first. The novel was an instant success and directly contributed to the survival of the Singer brothers. In the summer of 1932, in connection with a theatrical staging of his book, Israel Joshua visited the United States for several months. The stage adaptation of *Yoshe Kalb*, starring the famous actor Maurice Schwartz, was to become the greatest hit in the history of the Yiddish theater.

Bashevis was enchanted by the mysticism of this story, its unique atmosphere, and, of course, its love plot. At the time he was already working on his first novel, *Satan in Goray*, which in turn was to astonish his brother. Printed in installments in *Globus* in 1933, it was called "a historical legend." An emissary of the prophet Sabbatai Zevi appears in a small town in the Lublin region toward the end of the seventeenth century, causing messianic madness. The still-living memories of Chmielnicki's massacres unite with images of erotic exaltation aroused by the newcomer's influence.

Singer became a member of the Jewish Writers' Club and in time of the P.E.N. Club too. In the great cities of Europe people were dancing the latest dances: the Charleston, the foxtrot, whatever they were called. To young Bashevis they seemed like dances at the edge of the grave. He sensed the coming of inevitable annihilation. He felt that nothing could protect the Jewish Pompeii. The atmosphere of doom was growing. "One did not have to be particularly prescient to foresee the hell that was coming." He wanted to flee Poland. He thought it was his only chance for survival.

Hitler became chancellor of the German Reich in January 1933. In March he began persecuting Jews. On May 10 the first public burning of books took place, under the slogan "Standardizing the culture." In Poland, in April 1934, the ONR, National Radical Camp, was founded. Israel Joshua had been living in New York since 1933. He began looking for ways to bring his younger brother over.

One year later, in April 1935, Isaac Bashevis Singer received a passport, an American visa, and money for the ocean crossing. He left Poland, never to return, yet always going back in his art.

He never wrote about the Holocaust. He prophesied it, and afterward he sometimes made his protagonists its victims. But he never wrote directly about what happened in Poland during World War II.

A few days after the war broke out, the Tereshpol Minor town crier read aloud in the market square an order that all Jews were to leave the town within twenty-four hours. . . .

The Lublin road was jammed with wagons, carts, and pedestrians. . . .

The Poles who lived in the town acted as though what was going on was none of their affair. They went unconcernedly about their daily chores. Markevich, the slaughterer, slit the throat of a pig; Dobush, the butcher, went on with his corn-threshing and apple-gathering. Antek Liss, the bootmaker, left his bench to stroll over to the shop of Mottel, the leather dealer, and propose that the stock of leather be sold to him for a third of its value.

"They'll take it away from you anyway," he announced. "And there are rumors that they're going to kill all the Jews." He drew his finger suggestively across his gullet. "K-k-k-k!"

The Jewish housewives ran to their gentile neighbors to wail and sob, but the gentiles were too busy to listen to them. They were occupied with sifting flour, putting up preserves, churning butter, making cheese. The older women sat spinning flax, while the children played with dogs and cats or dug in the ground for worms. They could get along very well without the Jews.

The year was 1914.

Reb Dan's wagon drew up alongside the cart on which Jekuthiel the watchmaker sat, the tools of his trade piled around him. He looked at the rabbi and smiled sadly.

"*Nu*, rabbi?" he said.

It was clear what he meant was: Where is your Lord of the Universe now? Where are His miracles? Where is your faith in Torah and prayer?

"*Nu*, Jekuthiel," the rabbi answered. What he was saying was: Where are your worldly remedies? Where is your trust in the gentiles? What have you accomplished by aping Esau?

How many similar scenes were repeated a quarter century later?

THE STRANGER

Isaac Bashevis Singer was thirteen years old when he began reading in Polish. Before then it was a foreign language to him, even though his ancestors had lived in the country on the Vistula for centuries. As an eighteen-year-old he studied Polish grammar and knew it well enough to read Polish easily. He did his translations from German into Yiddish with the assistance of Polish versions. In his immigration papers for the United States Singer wrote that he knew how to speak and write Polish.

He often mentioned a literary text that he supposedly wrote in Polish, sometimes calling it a poem in prose, sometimes a short story. More often he confessed that he had trouble speaking the language of Adam Mickiewicz, Poland's greatest poet. The soft consonants gave him the most trouble.

Despite centuries of common history, he felt like a foreigner in Poland, like a stranger, conscious of the profound spiritual gulf dividing the two peoples. In his article "Jews and Poles—They Lived Together for 800 Years, But They Didn't Get to Know Each Other," he wrote: "Of the three million Jews living in Poland, approximately two and a half million were unable to write the simplest letter in Polish and made crude mistakes in speaking it. Polish meant as little to them as Chinese. I myself was born in a family that had lived in that country since the time of my great-grandfather's grandfather, but my father knew scarcely two words of Polish and it would never have crossed his mind that there was something peculiar about this."

In the 1931 census more than 80 percent of Jews declared that Yiddish was their mother tongue. It is impossible to reconstruct how many of them actually spoke Polish. It is impossible to determine how fluently they spoke this language.

Maybe Cyprian Norwid wasn't his writer, or Stefan Żeromski, or Bolesław Prus. In the final analysis, it wasn't in these Polish writers' language that he prayed. But Warsaw was indisputably his city. He was never lost in it.

The topographical accuracy of his literary walks is astonishing. It is as if a city map had imprinted itself somewhere in his memory, creating the underlying pattern of a literary scene, a map of the city he had most deeply internalized, the place he sometimes called home and sometimes fatherland. On Krochmalna Street, Twarda, Śliska, Gnojna, where "a familiar stench rose from the wide gutters, filled with slops," and young people with disheveled *peyess*, dressed in long gaberdines, walked to a nearby prayer house, with volumes of the Talmud under their arms.

A horse-drawn omnibus traveled the route from the Wiedeński Station to Praga on the right bank of the Vistula.

Żabia Street was where the hatters lived.

To find a jeweler, you went to Chłodna Street.

The big piece goods stores were on Gęsia.

Demonstrators with red flags preferred Dzika.

On Franciszkańska were dealers in leather goods and textiles, prayer books and pens.

Streetcars were red. Street lights were greenish blue. The cupolas of the Orthodox churches were gold.

The roasted potatoes sold on Świętokrzyska Street from a small portable oven were an infallible harbinger of winter.

And on Nalewki, as in the old days, one could get everything: shirts and wicker ware, cotton and buttons, parasols and silk, chocolate and plush, caps and threads, jewelry and tallithim. Street vendors praised their potato pancakes, roasted peas, slices of watermelon. A ragpicker with a sack slung across his shoulder bought up saucepans, griddles, old shoes, trousers, hats, rags.

His characters lived on those same streets. For example, the heroes of *The Family Moskat*: Meshulam Moskat lived on Grzybowska Street, Abram Szapiro on Złota, Asa Heshel on Pańska. Are they still living there, on the pages of the book of the world? If so, then in No. 12 Krochmalna Street, Reb Rafał, the shoemaker, still sits in his cellar, hammering away with his hammer. One can still have inexpensive soles put on in his shop. In old miser Zaruski's apartment on Marszałkowska, near Próżna Street, a treasure in a safe awaits a lucky locksmith. A beggar still sings a mournful ballad about the sinking of the *Titanic*. In the courtyard of the prayer house on Gnojna Street, stinking of urine, stand boxes full of pages torn from the sacred books.

At dawn the faithful gather for prayer. The cantor intones in his high voice: "Blessed be Thou, our God, and God of our fathers, God of Abraham, God of Jacob, God of Isaac. . . ."

Singer's world is not a sepia photograph. His scrupulousness in recording addresses, houses, places, real forms carries over to colors, sounds, even smells, the memory of which was "concealed in the deepest corners of my soul." His world is unusually sensual.

The Magician of Lublin, one of his literary heroes, rode into Warsaw across the Praga bridge. The air smelled of "fresh baking, coffee, horse manure, smoke from trains and factories." Max Barabander from *Scum* remembered the smell of Warsaw from bygone years as "a mixture of lilacs, sewage, tar, winds sweeping in from the Praga forests, and a something that had no name."

It was not only the city that emitted its own odor. Every street had one. The chronicler of Warsaw Jewry put together his own catalog of smells. Krochmalna was the stench of rubbish, sewage, the gutter. Gnojna, the stink of oil, horse manure, soap, and axle grease. Grzybowski Square was the smell of the marketplace: overripe fruit, citrus, or a mixture of something sweet and tarlike. In the synagogues it smelled of dust and wax.

Next to the monument to King Zygmunt, Singer allowed his heroes to see the old castle of the Polish kings, occupied by the Russian governor-general. He observes a military band and Russian flags fluttering on balconies on holidays. He looks at the Russian signboards and street names. He sees the Polish city enslaved.

In 1918 Russian military men were replaced by Polish military men: policemen, soldiers, officers in four-cornered hats who were "always fastening their buttons while giving military salutes." The Russian signs were painted over, replaced by Polish ones. It was at that time that people began listening to the radio, telephones stopped being a novelty, taxis appeared on the streets.

Singer did not write much about Poland's having achieved independence in 1918, after 123 years of subjugation. It was not *his* independence. He felt like a subtenant in his own city. But in the autumn of 1939, not long after the Germans attacked Warsaw, he began publishing a series of historical articles in the Jewish daily *Forward*, whose heroes were Poles: Stanisław August Poniatowski, Adam Mickiewicz, Ignacy Paderewski, and also Berek Joselewicz, a yeshiva student who fought side by side with "the national hero Tadeusz Kościuszko in a struggle for the liberation of Poland" in the late eighteenth century. This cannot have been pure chance.

There is no doubt that he knew the history of Poland. He remembered the names of the Polish kings of the Piast and Jagiello dynasties, Stefan Batory and Jan Sobieski. He moved freely in the thickets of partitions, uprisings, and rebellions. He mentioned and flawlessly associated the names of Jan Kiliński, Bartosz Głowacki, General Zajączek, Jarosław Dabrowski—all military heroes—or the old Polish aristocratic families: the Zamoyskis, Radziwiłłs, Czartoryskis. His Jewish protagonists knew the way to the elegant cafés—to the Lourse, the Semadeni, or the Ziemiańska—just as well as they knew the routes to their houses of worship. He knew the names of the outdoor theaters and their stars and also the repertoires of the opera and its favorites.

He was not mistaken when he called the women's section of the Warsaw prison Serbia, an alcohol-fueled stove a Primus, and dogs in the countryside Burek. He listed the stations on the Warsaw–Otwock line in perfect order. Polish sayings came to his and his characters' minds: "He who is meant to be hanged will not drown," or, "Kielbasa is not for dogs." He remembers other proverbs that were embroidered on wall hangings: "God rewards the early riser" and "A guest in the home—God in the home." He never forgot the children's song "A cat climbed up the fence. . . ."

He had most likely visited Poles in their homes; on several occasions he describes the typical interior of a simple family's house, with a table in the middle of the room surrounded by chairs, deer antlers on the wall, a cage with a canary in it, a sewing machine, and a likeness of Christ with a curly beard and a crown of thorns on his head, above which burns a small red lamp.

A Polish general's home looks like a museum. Faces of Polish national heroes gaze from the walls; everywhere there are medals, decorations, mounted heads of stuffed animals, revolvers, and sabers.

He insisted that one must write only about what one knows best. He had reason to do so. It is hard to resist the impression that the majority of the Gentiles who inhabit his world are the product of a demonic imagination.

Singer's Jews are authentic. Not only the Hasidim, the Orthodox, the traditionalists but also those who have moved away from their faith and are even seeking to flee their Jewishness through assimilation. His Poles frequently remind one of the heroes of trashy popular novels. His modern characters are an exception.

The typical Polish man according to this scheme would look like this: a member of the landed gentry or a prince, perhaps even a descendant of Polish kings. With a small blond goatee. Rarely sober. Usually he has drunk up his entire estate. He gets up at night and drinks vodka through a straw from a pitcher (!). He is entangled in a series of judicial proceedings, all of which he has lost. He has also lost at cards. An old bachelor who seduces village girls, with whom he conceives bastard children. Or a widower, a womanizer. An apoplectic tyrant. Proud and haughty. A crank. Sometimes consorting with unclean spirits. Seen with a woman demon on a horse. Sometimes faithful to love unto death.

It is hard to believe that the purest of the women whom Singer ever described, Wanda, from *The Slave*, was born and grew up in a primitive, dirty, degenerate village, a place whose horrors he described with particular vividness. This horrifying vision of the sub-Carpathian Polish countryside from the time of the writer Henryk Sienkiewicz's trilogy, immediately after the Chmielnicki pogroms, undoubtedly testifies to the extraordinary inventiveness of the author's pen, but how well does it accord with facts?

In a cow shed the peasants hold a Jewish slave, a runaway from the Cossacks, whom they have purchased at the market. They want to kill him as the priest encourages them to do. Shameless and deceitful, they live like animals. The women's clothing is vermin-infested, and their hair is full of matted clumps. They speak Polish poorly, grunt like animals, howl, and laugh wildly. They copulate in public, get pregnant, frequently miscarry, and throw the dead babies into a stream. The shepherds are a group of crippled, half-idiotic beings; they stink of urine, are devastated by diseases and vodka.

Singer's picture of the Jewish town is not idealistic either, but its coloration is not as intensely and unambiguously black. Descriptions of filth, superstition, hypocrisy are balanced by demonstrations of a certain degree of civilization. The Jews gossip, cheat, and steal, but there are good, honorable, righteous servants of God among them. In the Polish swamp only one pearl shines: Wanda.

The Slave was not translated into Polish during Singer's lifetime. The novels *The Manor* and *The Estate* were well received. "Had I described Poles unrealistically, they would have ripped me to shreds . . ." he said.

PART TWO

Here

⁋| Silence |⁋

EASTERN POLAND, 1992   He looks perfectly ordinary. Gray. He stands in the road in Bełżec, not far from the former extermination camp. He keeps Jewish gold teeth in a chest of drawers, wrapped up in a handkerchief. How many of them can there be? Several, a dozen? He has counted, but there are more and more of them. At first he used a riddle framed with four boards to sift the earth. Now he has a special Japanese device for metal detecting. All sorts of objects emerge: metal cups with Jewish lettering, saucers, shot glasses, ladies' compacts, safety razors.

"The ones from Bełżec," a stoker from Tomaszów tells me, "are millionaires, thanks to the Jewish corpses."

The camp grounds, the earth littered with red bricks, birches, pine trees, some old specimens and also some very spindly ones, probably planted not long ago. A white chapel. Sometimes they find bones too, if they have pieces of metal in them.

"In this place, from February to December 1942, there was a Nazi extermination camp in which more than six hundred thousand Jews from Poland and other countries in Europe met a martyr's death, along with fifteen hundred Poles who were murdered for helping Jews."

Sobibór also had a camp. When people looked for gold there after the war, they found crucifixes too.

"The Jews were also people, and there were good Jews too."

"The Jews were people who wanted to live."

"If it weren't for the Germans, the Jews would have strangled us."

"We had turnips growing during the war, and the Jews ate them all up at night."

Where do they lead to, those roads in my country, paved with the stones from Jewish cemeteries?

In Kock there is a man whose entire cellar is made of Jewish tombstones, but lately he has stopped bragging about this and he would not let me come inside.

In the Lublin region, in the little Jewish towns, there are traces, there is a sense of something missing, the erasure of a certain important element of prewar daily life. The old men in the market squares of Kock, Lubartów, Goraj tell stories about smart aleck Rajch, who owned a beer hall on Zamojska Street (a Miss Grossman fell in love with him, to her sorrow, and shot herself); about Josele the tailor, whose sewing machine sang Hasidic melodies; about the rabbi's wife from Kurów (the milkman, a Gentile, was secretly in love with her); and about Bojm the baker, whose breads—pumpernickel, whole wheat, and rye—were purchased with gratitude.

Roman Kowal from Bilgoraj wants to record the voices of the dead. He is not ready yet; he doesn't have an appropriate machine; he'll have to wait until he retires. But how will he understand those Jewish voices? They always spoke so strangely.

A cuckoo called out while they were being marched under escort to Zwierzyniec in November 1942. It cuckooed for a long time, and they thought it foretold many more years, a long life for them all. They did not know that their remaining time could be measured only in minutes. They were shot on a sandy hillside before they could even board the train. A few of them hid in villages. One even stayed in hiding for a long time after the war, because the people who hid him wanted to extract more money from him. For some three or four months he didn't know that the war was over.

People say that in the barracks at the Lubelska and Kościuszko streets crossroads where the Biłgoraj Jews were housed before they were loaded onto the trains, the floor was completely covered with torn-up money. That's the scene that supposedly greeted those who entered there. I didn't meet a single eyewitness, but a lot of people told me about this.

"It was green with dollars," they said. "The Jews destroyed them, ripped them up; they wouldn't leave any for us."

"They spoke real funny in that jargon of theirs, those little Jews. Shopkeepers, restaurant owners, watchmakers. They yelled, *'Oy vay!'* and *'Gevalt!'* They adored plush fabrics. Our washerwomen did their laundry for them and rinsed it in the river. There are no secrets from a priest, a doctor, or a washerwoman. Cleanliness was not one of their sins. Jewish sweat was not like our sweat. It smelled different—of garlic, onions."

Stefania K. remembers. She remembers the Biłgoraj Jews.

They were millionaires and paupers. Shopkeepers with tiny haberdasheries and potentates who traded in timber under contract to Zamoyski, the big landowner. There were those who had mastered the Japanese market, made a fortune in the timber trade with Russia and even farther afield—Persia and Mongolia. They bought and sold horses, grain, poultry, timber and timber futures, in addition to the traditional sieves.

In January 1942 a Jewish family was given a monthly allotment of 2.12 pounds of bread, 7 ounces of sugar, 2 ounces of soap, and a little over a quart of kerosene.

Three deportations to the extermination camp in Bełżec were carried out in the spring and autumn of 1942. Among the murdered were: Lipa Wakszul, groceries; Josef Rapaport, haberdashery; Chaskiel Kandel, kerosene products; Chaskiel Albersfeld, Jakub Grynapel, Ben Zion Rozenbaum, and Judka Szarf. . . .

Out of the five thousand Biłgoraj Jews, four thousand were murdered by the Germans. Most of the others perished from hunger and disease. Only a handful survived. No Jews live in Biłgoraj today.

When the Germans decided to liquidate the little ghetto, says N., they led the Jews to the attic. Tailors, furriers, shoemakers, watchmakers. They ordered them to stand naked at the window. From there they were thrown out, and a soldier fired at them from below. They fell. They flew like birds.

I talk about Jews with children, for example in Piaski, with children who are playing in the Jewish cemetery, which has been turned into a playground and amusement park. They know very little; they understand nothing. They say the Jews were some kind of people who didn't believe in our God, spoke a funny Polish, and no longer exist. A characteristic feature of Jews was that they had gold teeth. Lots of gold teeth. A nomadic people, but we don't like them.

A coffin maker's. I decide to order an oak coffin in order to start a conversation with the owner. A Jew? There was one here, but he didn't admit it. People looked for jewelry in their cemetery. "You're surprised? Don't you know what a Jew has on him? Gold!"

Mr. Boguś from Tomaszów:

"What do I remember?"

They shot them like crows. He would gulp down a shot of vodka and go back to shooting. And then another drink. Until it was over.

A Jewish woman wrapped in a down quilt in the marketplace.

The furrier took money to save them, and then he himself killed the Jewesses. He drank himself to death on grain alcohol in the barn. Justice was done.

In Piaski, when I ask who used to live here, I hear: "It used to be a Jewish town, but now it's Polish." There's something about the voice of that woman sweeping the street in front of a formerly Jewish shop (today it is still a paint store that one enters by descending the same stone steps). There's something in her voice that horrifies me and makes me look mournfully at the red geraniums blooming in the windows of this town.

The first time I visited the Lublin region it was autumn. The leaves were turning red. I saw that world, the remains of that world, in the twofold majesty of death.

After the war the Jewish cemeteries were ransacked over

and over again in search of gold. Today chickens strut about in the Jewish cemeteries and drunks drink vodka there straight from the bottle.

The first bomb that fell in Kock struck a pear tree near the rabbi's house. The rabbi and his whole family were standing under the pear tree, wrapped in down quilts. They were ripped to shreds. The rabbi's hand was hanging on a nearby fence; it could be identified by the ring with a green stone. Its fingers pointed toward heaven.

The synagogue in Kock didn't catch fire in the town conflagration during which the church burned down. The Poles said at the time: "Your God is more merciful." But immediately afterward the Germans demolished the synagogue and killed all the Jews.

Mr. D. from Goraj used to share a school bench with a Jewish girl, a printer's daughter; he was ashamed of this. But they got along well with each other; she would give him her matzoh in exchange for his roll.

"They used to say to the Jews, 'Bring me some marbles, and I'll see to it that no one beats you up.' They sang beautifully, they counted well—by bending and straightening their fingers. In the movie theater they were in the majority; they used to eat pumpkin seeds and spit out the shells. The seats closest to the screen cost forty groschen, so a Jewish boy would hold a Jewish girl in his lap and pay only that much.

"They were masters at selling: 'Lady, you look familiar, what's your name, where are you from?' "

"For us they were real live people. It was fun with them; at night all the shops were open so the merchandise would sell. But should they come back? No. By now we've grown accustomed to being without them."

Cemetery Street leads to the cemetery in Frampol. It is surrounded by a fence. About forty gravestones have survived. The oldest is from 1857. Some have been stolen; the remainder are resting in the earth. "The soil here," the *Dictionary of the Kingdom of Poland* informs us, "is clay, mixed with sand or in places completely sandy, and stones and flints of various dimensions are found in it occasionally. The topography is mostly flat."

Frampol and Goraj were famous for weaving.

Dzików, where Isaac Bashevis Singer's father lived after he moved away from Warsaw, and where he died, is a suburb of Tarnobrzeg today. It is on the Vistula River. In the seventeenth century the Tarnowski family built a fortified castle there and a Dominican church. On May 20, 1678, a miraculous icon of the Savior's mother was transferred to this church; earlier it had hung in the castle's chapel. The castle was on a hill; it commanded a magnificent view of the Vistula and the city of Sandomierz. Its distinctive feature was the tower with its old clock. A valuable library and a picture gallery, with a book collection of seven hundred Polish works or works about Poland, a complete set of the astronomer Hevelius's writings illustrated with artistic woodcuts, rare editions of the poet Mikołaj Rej, numerous manuscripts. Many paintings, among them: Titian's "Sorrowful Mother of God," Rembrandt's "Cossack Horseman," a landscape by Claude Lorraine.

In the only surviving mikvah in Poland, in Zamość, on Zamenhof Street, there is now a discotheque.

When the angel flew over Chełm, carrying two sacks of souls, he got caught on the church steeple's spire and dumped out all the stupid souls from his ripped sack into that town.

In Chełm, the proverbial town of fools, there is not a single Jew. Before the war Jews accounted for half of the town's population. In the thirties they included: 380 shopkeepers, 61 merchants, 37 owners of tenement houses, 20 tailors, 17 bakers and confectioners, 14 industrialists, 9 barbers, 8 teachers, 8 doctors, 8 dentists, and as many accountants, watchmakers, clerks, locksmiths, blacksmiths, 7 millowners, 3 owners of brickworks, 3 hotel proprietors, 2 beer hall owners.

In Chełm there were two synagogues: an old sixteenth-century synagogue and a new one dating from the beginning of the nineteenth century. Today, instead of prayers, the noise of a merchandise exchange issues from the great synagogue of the Hasidim of these parts. The banking hall where transactions are concluded is in the room where the Holy Torah lay in years gone by.

The cemetery at the intersection of Kolejowa and Staroś-cińska streets was devastated by the Germans; they used the gravestones to build roads. Even after the war people collected the stones to use for foundations. Today it is difficult to discern the traces of Jewish graves in this meadow with its few trees. I light a candle in front of one of them, perhaps the only one that remains intact.

The largest Jewish cemetery in Lubartów was in the center of the town, not far from the synagogue and the Jewish community's buildings. It survived the occupation; after the war it was converted into a children's playground and soccer field. Right beside it are the municipal toilets. Today it is a place where one can drink, play cards, and get punched in the face.

The other cemetery was at a distance from town. It dates from the beginning of the last century. Now a housing cooperative's apartment buildings, constructed in the early seventies, stand there on Cicha Street. During the excavation for the buildings' foundations workers dug up human skulls and bones. A couple of years ago they erected a monument made of Jewish gravestones, which are still being destroyed. Students from the nearby school break empty wine and beer bottles against the tombstones; they often use the wall as a substitute toilet.

People point out a house not far from the marketplace in Lubartów; the last Lubartów Jew, the shammes Matys Zoberman, son of Berek, is said to live there. A shopwindow: ladies' tailoring, across from the playground. Then I find out that the old Jewish cemetery was on this spot.

The door is opened by a short, tired woman, her hair ruined by a permanent, with gold earrings: Mrs. Gdul.

"Pan Marian? You're too late; he's dead."

Her grandson promises to bring me a color photograph of Pan Marian. He looks as if he were alive, lying stretched out in his open coffin.

"He didn't want to cause anyone any trouble. 'Bury me and make it level with the ground, so there isn't a trace,' he said. He saw how people desecrated the graves of his friends. He buried them himself, said kaddish for them. He was the last.

"He used to go from cemetery to cemetery. He wept in them. Because there would be broken tablets in one place, gravestones smeared with colored paint somewhere else. He was afraid of that. On his last day he begged me, 'Don't bother with a grave for me; let there be no grave.' "

When the war ended, Matys Zoberman weighed seventy-seven pounds. His parents had perished in Treblinka; he himself had managed to escape from the train. He went back to Skoki in Radzymin County, to his native village. But someone denounced him immediately, and he was sent to Majdanek, then to Skarżysko and to several camps in Germany. When he regained some strength, he made his way back to his native region once more. The Germans were gone by then. Thirty-two Jews returned; they had been with peasants or with the partisans or in Russia. But they all stayed only for a short time, and then they went their separate ways. Only Matys remained; he settled down in Lubartów in the house of one of his relatives. People kept telling him, "Run away," so he went to Tel Aviv, to his family. He came back after a couple of months; he couldn't get adjusted. People wouldn't leave him in peace, so he tried running away once more, this time to America, to a cousin. But he couldn't sleep there. He came home again. And he didn't travel any more. Apparently there is no better place, he thought. And he stayed.

"He toiled for so many years here. On January 15, 1991, we buried him in the Gdul family grave; he was friends with my mama, he was like a father to me."

The house they live in is a grain storage shed that used to be owned by Jews. The oil mill was next door; there are still signs of it. Pan Marian made it his home.

"As for Pan Marian, you could only compare him with Jesus," says Pani Ewa. "All he wanted was that others should have the best possible life and that he should cause the least amount of trouble. 'Bury me in the Jewish cemetery in Lublin, and make my grave level with the earth.' He used to ask forgiveness for having survived; maybe he'd gotten accustomed to the camps? He traveled to Lublin frequently, to the cemetery, to pray. He was a gravedigger and mourner for his remaining Jewish brethren."

The Torah lay in its oilcloth cover on the little table in the room that he rented from the Gduls, next to the wardrobe with its oval mirror and a chest of drawers. Pani Ewa, even though she works as a court attorney, had no idea what it was. It had little wooden handles protruding from it, she remembers that. Only after Pan Marian's death did people come from Lublin and take the Torah to the museum.

Pan Marian's room had a private entrance; he entered the Gduls' home from the courtyard. Still, he would often sit with them all day long. They would talk or be silent. Out front, on the main entrance, someone had scratched a Star of David with a nail. It was a deep gouge; Mrs. Gdul had to use a lot of paint to cover it over, but even so it still showed.

The director of the court asked Pani Ewa: "What, exactly, is that Zoberman to you? There's a Jew who lives in my apartment block, but I wouldn't shake hands with him."

They didn't post any death notices or announcements about the funeral so that no one who wasn't invited would show up. Even so, there were a few gawkers. Someone said a prayer in Yiddish. What difference does it make what language it was in? It's all the same pleading with God.

"He remained with us. He is lying in our family grave. With our grandfathers. In a Catholic cemetery. There was always a place for him in our home. The last Jewish shammes from Lubartów."

———

Józef S. from Frampol talks about the Jews.

That they were in trade, but hard work wasn't their specialty.

That several of them had horses and leased a wagon.

That the Germans drove them to the Jewish cemetery and brought back suitcases full of dollars and watches.

That the pits were dug deep and wide, conveniently.

That the Germans ordered them to jump into the pit and that was the end of that.

Józef S. from Frampol can't forgive himself for not having figured out the system in time.

Mietek M. kept an entire family in his attic.

One woman in the village took the cows out to pasture; they pretended she was the farmer's ward.

Stanisław S.'s buildings were brick; it was easy for him, they were fenced in. No one knew who was inside.

All of them made fortunes. They sent them money for the rest of their lives. And the packages—what delicacies. They educated their children. And what nicely furnished homes they have!

Jan P. does not expect a reward because he didn't do anything for them. He doesn't expect any punishment either. Once, when he was working as a lineman, he caught a Jew, but he didn't turn him in. He let him go. People like that were in power later. He thinks one should be careful even now about whom one talks to. A journalist from Warsaw . . . "Do you have any documents, miss, that prove you are a Pole?"

———

Maybe Frampol doesn't exist anymore; maybe all that's left of it is my story, wrote Isaac Bashevis Singer.

Why should they remember? Is there an obligation? They iron their curtains to welcome Jesus Christ at Christmastime. Soon they will decorate the Christmas tree and sing carols to the Infant. Those others are not needed; they are strangers, with their unknown lives, their vain deaths. Their cemeteries, synagogues, prayers serve no purpose. "Why should we have money for other people's dead when we don't have any for our own living?" asks a blue-eyed farmer's wife.

弓‖ THE ORCHARD ‖彡

LEONCIN, CENTRAL POLAND, 1992   He gave me a visa to a world whose existence I had to believe in on his word alone. I searched desperately for confirmation of the reality of the stage props of that time. I searched for witnesses, if only for trees or stones that bore their names. More than half a century had passed since the days when people crowded into the synagogues to pray on the Sabbath. I was late, so only the last survivors or shadows received me. I did not hesitate to speak with them.

Why did I want to touch the places that he had touched, among which he had lived, which marked the rhythm of his daily existence? In what way was this journey supposed to change me? How much did it manage to change my image of the world and country where all this had taken place?

The Singer family left Leoncin in 1907. No one remembers them. They cannot remember. Recently people have wanted to name the local school after Isaac Bashevis.

How did Leoncin, a village several hundred yards from the northern boundary of the Kampinos Forest and not quite a mile and a quarter from the Vistula River, come into being? Some say that the local squire, Leon Chrystowski, sold the Jews the sandy, nonarable land and helped them build their settlement. Out of gratitude they named it after him.

Daniela Różycka was born in Leoncin. She was seventeen when the war broke out. She knew everyone here.

"There was a Singer in Leoncin, but he was a maker of leather boot uppers, not a rabbi. There might have been some kind of family connection, but I'm not sure. They called him Lipa. He didn't make boots; he only sewed the uppers. On the other hand, your Singer most likely lived in Radzymin and his parents lived in Leoncin a very long time ago. You know, miss, it's hard for me to say, because the Jews didn't use surnames, just Abramka, Mrs. Josek, Mrs. Moszek. I'd have to reconstruct their surnames now.

"Hereabouts the land almost everywhere used to belong to Jews. This street was the main and only street in Leoncin. It didn't have a name. It was sandy; in the autumn the mud was terrible. Sand and mud. Once all the houses here were wooden. Only they were covered with reeds, so they looked stuccoed. Now there are more brick buildings. Jews lived on this street, in almost all the houses.

"There were about one hundred families in Leoncin, or perhaps there weren't quite that many. The people lived in poverty, in great poverty. When I recall the conditions in which some of them lived, it's unthinkable. Even on bare earthen floors. I knew some like that, and the children, I remember, gathered berries in the forest, and that's what they lived on. It's appalling, what poverty, not even a decent bed, nothing. But they had to live. In the summer they would go to the wealthier farmers and take the cattle out to pasture in order to earn money for potatoes for the family for the winter. A two-pound bread cost twenty to twenty-five groschen, depending on the kind of flour; day-old was cheaper. A roll was five groschen. Kerosene was thirty-eight. Vodka was two zlotys ten for a half liter. And a woman day worker, when she went out to do laundry, because there were no businesses here or industry, only farms—well, if they hired her to work in the fields, they would pay one zloty twenty per day, plus dinner. There were pork chops and ham, of course, but who had money for that? The butcher took everything he had to Warsaw; here all he could sell were giblets, bacon, ribs, kielbasa, headcheese, tripe. Who could afford ham? Ham was for Easter. Today people complain, but they also have different palates. I won't say anything, but the Jews took good care of themselves. They bought a lot of fish; they ate a lot of vegetables. We children didn't like those fish cutlets that Abramka brought us for treats.

"She would eat in our house too. She would always ask, 'Was the pan greased with butter?'

" 'Yes,' Mama would say.

"They both knew it was greased with lard, but the sin would be on Mother. We lived together peacefully. I never heard my parents say anything bad about Jews. Our neighbor even sought advice about personal problems, and her husband, when he quarreled with her, would run to complain to Papa.

"There was a marketplace here before the war. There were fairs every other Monday, twice a month. Only animals were traded; horses, cows, pigs. This is where we lived, only not in this house but in a wooden one. Next came Nowakowski's Polish store. The midwife lived in the Nowakowskis' house. Beyond them was Mrs. Janowska. It was Janowska who sold her place to Obrączka the tailor. Next, a tiny little house; that was the Ryśkiewiczes'. Then there was the other Lipa and also a certain Josek. He had a shoemaker's shop, and here is where the tailor lived, the shoemaker on the top floor and the tailor in the middle. Well, next came Poles, the Wrzesiński family; that house is still standing, over there where you see that little shop. But they rented; it was a rental house. Both Jews and Poles lived there, all together, on the ground floor and upstairs. That big house, the yellow one, was Pawłowski's store, Polish. Farther on was the so-called Jewish tearoom, in that large wooden building on the left side of the street. They called it a tearoom; they didn't serve hard liquor, only some light wine, beer, soda, tea. And sweets: cakes, tea cakes, that is. When our people got a little drunk in the tavern, they would come here to brawl afterward. The tavern was on the corner, right next to the church.

"Behind the tearoom was a Jewish grocery. In the next house there were two small shops, both selling piece goods, Jewish. Farther on, Rafał's, a store that sold both piece goods and ready-to-wear clothing, also Jewish; that building is still standing. Next door the Pawłowskis', a private house; there was nothing there. Chryścianka had a large piece goods store, but Polish. There were more Jews engaged in trade. And also, out back, was the Jews' slaughterhouse. They slaughtered beef, kosher for themselves and the rest for the others. Whoever wanted bought. A shed; they lived there and sold there. There was also a tailor, but he was a Pole; he sewed to order. Then, even farther off, were a second slaughterhouse in a shed and a Jewish butcher shop; they sold a lot of kosher meat and so forth. And they peddled it in the villages. So-called Big Jankiel and Little Jankiel. Big Jankiel had only a stall, but Little Jankiel had a shop.

"Behind Little Jankiel's, out in back, was the temple. The large building was the wooden synagogue, and, beside it, the bathhouse. The rabbi, his name was Nagubin, lived in the synagogue; on the left side they prayed, and on the right he had one room and a kitchen. Nothing was left of those buildings. The rabbi had three daughters: the eldest, Hanka, and two younger ones. Hanka and I went to the same school; we used to sit together in class. We attended the Polish school, which had three grades and seven classes. There was no Jewish school; all the Jews went to school with us. Szmul the shoemaker lived in the house next to the rabbi's. Next came a Polish shop, Krawczak's, which sold groceries and sausage. Farther on Caban also had a Polish store, the last house in Leoncin.

"Our cemetery was over there, where it is now. There was no Jewish cemetery in Leoncin, only in Zakroczym. They had to go there to bury their dead. On the other side was Mośkowa's, a greengrocer's; they were elderly people. They did the selling themselves, on the corner. Next was a large wooden building, Sztolcman's Jewish bakery. And apartments. Inside the courtyard was a market, a commercial market. People would come from Zakroczym, and our Jews would bring out tables and lay out trousers, skirts, shirts to sell. The Jews stood around with barrels of herrings, lots of barrels, and others came from Zakroczym to sell caps. They hung those caps on the wall of the first building. Rumianek lived there, but later he moved closer to the center, next to Szyja. Next was Mendelke Bajłowicz, the father. The son ran the teahouse; his name was also Bajłowicz. Over here was Majerek Kania, a tailor, he sewed really cheap ready-to-wear clothes, sturdy twill trousers, twill work clothes; they sold all those things at the market. Now it's half the size. A lot of people used to come, people selling furniture, coopers; the shoemakers from Zakroczym would hang their shoes on poles. There weren't any stores in the surrounding area, only in Leoncin; everyone went to the market when he needed something.

"No, I can't speak Yiddish. I used to understand a little, but they spoke Polish with us, almost everything in Polish. Among themselves they spoke Yiddish. The Jewish women were pretty, dark. And they cared about their appearance. When a couple were engaged, like the Bajłowicz daughter and

Jesionek, you could really see they were a couple, they took walks together so nicely. That one of them should get drunk, oh, no, there was none of that among the Jews.

"Were the majority Orthodox? No. Only a few Jews had *peyess*. The rabbi, maybe another three or four, Sztolcman, Bajłowicz. The rabbi always wore a hat. An intelligent man, you can't deny it, good-looking, cultured. They didn't dress like rich people, just average. The children ran away from here; they came back to their parents only right before the war. Already elegant, in fur coats.

"We got along very well with the Jews. My parents and I were at several of their parties. At a number of wedding ceremonies, in the courtyard, under the chuppah. At the parties after the weddings, when the parents went, the children raced to get there too. The Jews celebrated all their holidays very nicely, in a very cultured way, you can't deny it. The holy day began on Friday. Saturday was the Sabbath; they didn't do any work, everything was prepared beforehand. In winter a woman would come and light a fire for them; they were not permitted to do anything. Their food was prepared in one of the two Jewish bakeries, and a Polish woman, she was really poor, would pick it up and bring it back heated up from the bakery. She waited on them every Saturday.

"Were mutual relations good? Of course they were right here; I don't say it was the same everywhere, but among my neighbors and my family—yes. If they were to rise from their graves today, I wouldn't be afraid to look any one of them in the eye. I was never on bad terms with anyone, and they weren't on bad terms with me.

"During the war a lot of Jews fled Zakroczym and came to Leoncin. Artisans, the sort who used to come to the market here. Szulim the shoemaker, he made good shoes; even the Germans bought their shoes from him. Because during the occupation we had the German border command, the so-called customs officers. The border ran through the hills. We didn't have a ghetto; the ghetto was in Nowy Dwór. An entire staff of officers lived in our house, which was burned down in 1944. Like almost all the wooden houses. There were six rooms; the Germans occupied three, and we had three. Their offices were across the street. The Jews would come to wait on them; they shined their boots, did the housekeeping, took care of their horses. They had to answer to their every beck and call, of course, but in the beginning they weren't treated badly. The Jews were still here in 1942; they didn't drive them into the ghetto until later. They herded them into the market square and ordered them to walk. They kept back a number of artisans to work for them. The tailors Szulim and Obrączka were still sewing for them. But they drove out all the others in groups of four. We stood here in the courtyard while the Jewish women walked past; they said good-bye and sobbed. My God, what crying! Mama cried something awful. They called out, 'Mrs. Przedpełska, good-bye, good-bye'; they walked down the street saying good-bye. One officer was fond of a young Jewish girl. And she returned his affection. He had a wife, he was very well behaved, but he could watch her through binoculars from our window for hours on end. And as they were marching away, he too had tears rolling down his face. Everyone stayed in our courtyard; we were afraid to go out into the street.

"I was in the ghetto only once in my life, actually near the ghetto, once, at the dentist's. My husband used to bring bread there to his friends because my father-in-law had a bakery. He would give bread to those who had arranged for it. They were very poor there. Then they rounded up even those whom they had first kept back. They came for Obrączka too; they said he should get dressed. He told them, 'Wait a minute, just let me call the children.' He walked out and never came back. He went into hiding. He and his entire family survived."

In Leoncin itself no one survived in hiding.

Mr. Rutkowski speaks:
"Obrączka, the man from whom I bought my house, dabbled in trade from time to time. They were very good people, poor, really poor. When the Germans came later and took photographs of the houses and the people in the area in order to show what poverty there was, they took photographs of that little Jew's children. Another Jew, Lipka, was also a neighbor of mine. I was a shoemaker, and he was a shoemaker. I was young; he was an old man. A very good artisan and very honest. Everything he did was deluxe; he made such shoes that they were goodness itself for walking. He would get angry at his son because the son would do a sloppy job, do it faster, take in more money. I will never forget Lipka for as long as I live. Such kindheartedness, such a wise man. He couldn't read or write, only as much as he needed to sew shoes, but he spoke so wisely. When the Germans came, he knew he was going to perish, because they were rounding up the Jews, so he gave me a machine for making the shoelace holes in women's dress shoes. He gave me that machine as a gift. I will truly never forget that little Jew; what a good heart he had. Despite the fact that we Poles have always had it drilled into us that it was a Jew who crucified our Lord, he was like a father to me, with such kindheartedness. It was if he were saying good-bye. He never came back from the ghetto. His son would come over from Nowy Dwór from time to time. Sometimes he would collect some-

thing for the others too; he knew where the Jews were hiding around here. That Lipka was very religious, but Lipka's son was a bit of a rascal, because he was young. He would cook up kielbasa in a teakettle, and his mother would get angry; she even koshered the teakettle. A hooligan, but he was entertaining. I remember them.

"There were a lot of Jews in this region. There were more of them than of us. They had stores, or they walked from village to village and traded goods; they peddled goods, and that's what they lived on. They spoke Yiddish among themselves, and with us they spoke a broken Polish. But thanks to them, it was easier for me to communicate with the Germans later on. Because I was a little better than the other shoemakers in the district. Was I better than Lipka? Oh, yes, he only made ordinary shoes, but I made deluxe shoes too! Both women's and men's. I had a workshop and my own hired workers. But later, when communism came, it all fell apart; I had to liquidate it. They didn't allow it.

"The village boys tormented the Jews, that's for sure! During the holy days they would knock over their booths or hurl stones at them; they were real ruffians. They would toss dead animals into those booths, pour water inside or even something worse, even filth. When we bought this house, they tormented us too, thinking we were Jews. They would smear lard on the door handle or sneak some fatback in.

"The Jews were mainly tailors. My next-door neighbor, Gruszczyński—he's a Pole—his father was a well-known fine tailor. But those Jews, as soon as they sewed something, giddyap, they're off to the market, so long as it's cheap and in quantity. They had heads on their shoulders because they made money from sewing and from goods. They would buy fabric wholesale in Warsaw, sew, then sell it retail. They laughed at our Gruszczyński. It takes a day to sew decent trousers, but that little Jew, Obrączka, the one I bought the house from, he would sew eighteen pairs of pants in a single day. Sure, that was the way to sew. And he laughed. 'That Grruszczyński, he prresses, prresses, prresses. . . . ' But it's true, you have to have a head on your shoulders and be alert if you're going to manage to sew eighteen pairs. That one, he grew rich.

"They sent the Jews to Nowy Dwór. We even went to see them there. We could still buy things from them. The Germans let us in, and they wanted to sell because they had to have money. That's when I bought this house. Obrączka's wife had gold at her brother's, but he wasn't very willing to give it back. Yes, Obrączka survived. He was lucky; he had a Jewish head. He was quick-witted; the Germans came for him, the local ones, but by order of the police. 'Come along, you.' '*Oy*, all right, I'll just run and get my children.' He ran to his children and immediately fled into the forest and to Warsaw. We even carted some of his things to him. He survived. He managed somehow, with the aid of our parish priest. But very few survived, very few. Of all those whom I remember, only that one family."

Mrs. D. is eighty-nine years old. She is the same age as Isaac. She was born in Leoncin, but she doesn't remember the red-bearded rabbi or his children. She says that she knew all the Jews and where each one lived; she can show me. Also, where the synagogue was, the Jewish church. In the center of the main room was a carved chest in which they kept their gods.

But no one wants to know. She talks with her dog, who understands every word. She cries often.

Her father had a bakery, and he did very well under the Russians; later things were worse. She remembers how in 1914 the towers of their church collapsed; you could hear it from far away. She was still attending school. She used to love to listen to her grandfather's stories about mysterious disappearances in the bogs and swamps surrounding Leoncin. Later she left home. She earned her living by sewing in other people's houses.

"The Jews and the Poles lived together peacefully, without fighting. Then the Germans tortured both them and us; why? Tortured to death."

She doesn't want to talk about it anymore; it is too painful.

Memory has fled.

Mrs. D.'s orchard is in back of the house, and it is difficult to see it from the street. It is enclosed by a decrepit wooden fence. The orchard is returning to the wild. Only some dwarf apples and cherries still bloom. It is overgrown with gnarled hazelnut trees. Trees clearly demarcate a specific area. They stand scattered about on the edges of a weed-choked, empty space. Here is where the Singers' house and the synagogue once stood. Burdocks, thistles, wild chamomile, clover. As if nature wanted to honor the life that was lived here. It did not allow it to be replaced with another.

New tenants moved into the few surviving Jewish houses. They painted the worm-eaten boards a different color. They placed their own furniture in someone else's rooms, and now they celebrate their own lives here. The orchard maintains its silence.

⁊| Windows |⁊

RADZYMIN, CENTRAL POLAND, 1992   "Windows of cities select fragments of life minus all its complexity. Commotion and crowds have very little content. Windows in little towns are much wiser," he told an interviewer for the Polish weekly *Polityka*. His hero Nathan from "The Unseen" once "looked out of the window, and saw to his surprise that people were walking backward, and marveled at this. . . . Among those who passed, he recognized men who had long been dead. . . . Entire generations passed through the town, men and women with packs on their shoulders and staffs in their hands. He recognized, among them, his father and grandfather, his grandmothers and great-aunts."

"To Isaac Singer, an inhabitant of Radzymin, Nobel Laureate in Literature. 1991. The Society of Friends of Radzymin." The plaque has been cemented onto the wall of a building that stands where the old Jewish district once was. No one knows exactly how close it is to the rabbi's and his assistant's houses. Not much here resembles the provincial Jewish town in Warsaw Province, six and a half miles from the railway station in Tluszcz. Poor, sparsely settled, composed of two markets and a dozen or so unpaved streets. Formerly there was a tile factory in the town and another one that produced walking sticks. In addition to the parish church, there was an evangelical house of prayer and a synagogue.

The beautiful neoclassical palace, the jewel of Radzymin, which was erected by Princess Eleonora Czartoryska, no longer exists. The rabbi's cottage at the edge of the woods, where the Radzymin rabbi used to spend each summer, no longer exists. Few buildings in the market square remember the time when a Jewish woman, Mrs. Silberstein, ran a brothel there. Concrete has been poured over the old Jewish synagogue to create the foundations of a new housing block; a bus stop is located where the other synagogue once stood. Trees grow in the Jewish cemetery. The gravestones can be found in people's homes, in basements. They took them for foundations, for whetstones, to sharpen knives.

It is Sunday. People are coming out of church after high mass.

Leopold Wardak:

"I was born in 1920. So I saw all this from the perspective of a young man. Also the ghetto, which was only a few yards from my house.

"Those who insist that there is anti-Semitism in Poland are wrong. This is pseudo-anti-Semitism; it is hatred of Communist Jews, Communists of Jewish descent. Communist Poles are hated just as much. These people caused us great suffering, the Communists. If you're asking about ordinary Jews, well, we never especially liked them, but we lived together well enough. It's quite simple; we needed each other. A Jew, for example, would harness his horse, ride out to the squire in the village: 'Squire, sir, I have some goods for you.' And he'd sell them. Or he collected rags, carried around plates. It was a kind of teamwork.

"Would there be a Berek Joselewicz Street in an anti-Semitic country? Or a monument? Wałęsa went to Israel and apologized. But why did he apologize? For what?

"I know the problem of bad Jews from the inside; I used to work in the Ministry for Public Security, I, a Home Army member. All the directors there were Jews. They dominated the ministry. Everyone knows what harm those secret police agents did to us.

"Before the war there was no anti-Semitism, only some minor harassment. In my opinion, it's a matter of different personalities. A Jew liked to cheat, to trade; he didn't go out with Poles to drink vodka; he followed his own paths. They didn't mingle with Poles. They were separate. Our young men harassed them. For example, combating Jews was part of the National Unity Camp's program. 'Don't buy from a Jew.' They set up picket lines in front of their stores. On the other hand, the occupation was a plain tragedy. Dozens of Jews were shot in front of our eyes. If someone so much as walked outside the wire fence around the ghetto, they shot him. But the wires were loose, deliberately loose, so they would come out in search of food.

"Once, I remember, a German, Radke, was walking down the street and an ancient Jewess emerged right opposite him; he pulled out his pistol and fired, once, twice. She collapsed. He kept walking. And immediately she started yelping, like a dog. He'd shot her. About half an hour later he came back; a kid had told him, 'Mister, she's still alive,' so he finally finished her off. There were a lot of deaths like that.

"The liquidation of the ghetto. Early in the morning the Germans drove them all to a square near Reymont Street; I could see it clearly from my windows. They ordered the Jews to dig a pit, to carry the sick there, those who couldn't walk, and they shot them and then threw them into the pit. One of them from Jadów had no legs, he 'walked' on a little wheeled platform, propelling himself with his hands. A German shot him in the head at the edge of the pit, kicked him, and that was that. Later they exhumed the bodies from that spot and transported them to the Jewish cemetery; that was still during the occupation, in August '42. They loaded the rest of them onto freight trains."

Stefan Modzelewski:

"I am seventy-six years old, I live in Radzymin on Wysz-kowska Street. I am a cooper. I used to buy my hoops from Jews.

"Radzymin was a half-Jewish town. Warsaw Street was the boundary. The Poles lived to the east, and the Jews to the west, in the Old Town.

"Jews. They were very crowded. They worked as artisans, in trade, beef, fish, small businesses, tiny shops. They peddled goods in the countryside. There were no particular animosities in our mutual relations. The young people, as young people do, acted like hooligans, but there wasn't the kind of anti-Semitism that people are talking about now. The Jewish school was over there, where the Boreckis live now; it went through the fifth grade, and after that they attended school with us. Of course there was the National Democratic party, and I even belonged to it, but we didn't pull any stunts. In 1935 or '36 there was a convention of the entire province; the Jews didn't come out of their houses then. Not that anyone was being beaten up; they just didn't come out. Someone has been saying that Jews were killed near the smithy, but that's just gossip; I was there myself, and I would have known.

"There were two synagogues in Radzymin—one with

stuccoed walls across from the bus stop and the other a wooden one, where there are apartment houses now.

"What else did they do? They leased orchards in the country. Trade was in their hands for the most part. They were very frugal. Sure, they cheated, but that wasn't why they controlled trade. The Jews had their own wholesalers from whom Jewish shopkeepers got a discount, more than the Poles got. That's why the Poles couldn't compete with them. A Jew always sold for less because he paid less at the wholesaler's. That's why the slogan 'Don't buy from a Jew' was designed to help Poles. Another thing: The Jew was content with a grosz, but a Pole wants to earn fifty percent right away, and it's the same today. A Pole can't live on a lower income.

"During the war I was in the East; that's where I really got to know the Jews. After the Russians disarmed us, I made my way home through little Jewish towns where the Jews were running around with red armbands. With rifles in their hands."

"My name is Zygmunt Burdela. I was born in Radzymin in 1923 at Number twenty-five Piękna Street, which is now called May First Street. We had some property and a wooden house in which Jewish families lived. I remember families such as Dubek Izraelski, Szyja Epelbaum, Icek Lisowicki. They were poor Jews. For example, Szyja was a porter. He had three daughters: One was named Łajka, the second was Ryfka, and the third I don't remember. They didn't have money to pay the rent. There was a tenant protection season; from November 1 to April 1 you couldn't evict a tenant. When spring came, he would bring a couple of groschen, and then he wouldn't pay again. Another little Jew, Dubek Izraelski, was a cattle trader. He wasn't poor, but he didn't own any property. He lived in a house without any conveniences, very simply. Right before the war ritual slaughter was banned, but he continued to perform that kind of slaughter in secret. He was sentenced to ten months hard labor at the Bereza Kartuska camp. Icek Lisowicki was an upholsterer; he had four children and a tiny apartment. That's where he slept, where he brought those old couches, ottomans, sofas, where he hammered and did his repairs. The place was so infested with bedbugs that it was a pity even to look at it. He lived with us until the Germans came. Later I myself transported him to Pustelnik with my own cart. He was in the ghetto near Zielonka. I visited him there once: four families in a hundred-eighty-square-foot apartment. Later, they were taken to Warsaw. He escaped; he hid in the house of a woman in Marki who made carpet slippers. He spent the entire occupation with her. Once he came to our house, knocked on the window one evening. We were terrified; there was a death sentence for hiding Israelites. We couldn't keep him, it was too crowded, but my mother gave him supper. I led him to the stable, where he spent the night. He survived the war.

"I also had Jewish neighbors. Majlech, a shoemaker, lived nearby; he had two daughters and a son-in-law. Often I would walk outside at eleven at night and he would be hammering away; in the morning, when you got up, it was the same thing. The war came. Radzymin was bombed. The son-in-law fled to his father-in-law's, also right next door to us; a bomb fell right on them. It killed Mrs. Majlech; it killed her pregnant daughter, she lay there with her belly split open. The other daughter was also wounded. They were mainly poor Jews. Pinek had a shop on Piękna Street in a building that belonged to Mr. and Mrs. Chruścicki; he had a grain and foodstuffs wholesale warehouse on Peowiaków Street. He kept a chest with silver coins in that warehouse. The warehouse was bombed. And then the Germans dismantled the bombed buildings and moved the bricks to the airport. A brigade of Jews was assigned to this work; they got hold of the chest and began to quarrel because it was a lot of money. The Germans on patrol noticed the commotion, drove them off with clubs, and took the money.

"Cattle were slaughtered on my farm for the inhabitants of the ghetto. A certain Mieczysław Żmijewski, nicknamed Cium, was in charge of this. He had one Jewish assistant. They ran the operation twice a week. They would slit the cow's throat. The kosher butcher would come, inspect the meat, check out every part, and then it would go to the ghetto. Once they had hung the lungs and the liver on the wall and I hadn't managed to put anything away yet when Domaradzki walked in and asked what was going on. He was what we called a blue policeman, a member of the German-controlled Polish police force. 'You know best what's happening,' I answered. And he up and left. He didn't incriminate anyone.

"During the occupation I belonged to the volunteer fire department. Once when I was on duty, my colleague Stanisław Gorączkowski told me about some Jews who were murdered here in our Jewish cemetery. It was a family of nine people. One of these Jews was holding a little child in his arms. When the firing squad aimed at them, the one who was holding the child turned his back to them. A shot rang out. It hit him in the back. He fell on top of the child. A German walked over and killed them both."

A conversation around the table:

"I am Sójka, Wacek's twin brother. I know of a Jew who hid with the miller's wife near Siedlce. He used to treat me to moonshine and rye bread. He was a professional photographer, a tiny man, a dwarf. His shop was on Kilińskiego Street."

"The lumberyards were all in Jewish hands. When I was

seven, I was able to count those boards, but no Pole was able to count them. The Jews took advantage of that and cheated terribly. But they respected me because I could count."

"Them Jews had guts, but they was nasty."

"Those girls of theirs were very pretty, dark beauties. The Jews had their own sports association, the Maccabees. I didn't see any discrimination at all here. The hooligans harassed them, but that's normal.

"September tenth, 1939, on a Sunday, at three forty-five, German planes flew over and bombed Radzymin. Very accurately, particularly the synagogues. A period of hell began for the Jews."

"I met three people of Jewish descent who were outside the ghetto. One was the dwarf photographer who has already been mentioned. I was in the army in Kisielany; we were going to church, across a little bridge on the river, beside a water mill, and we accidentally met this little Jew, I don't remember his name—the little photographer. He took beautiful portrait photos, other types too; he photographed everyone. He lived in Mr. Księżyk's building."

"Mrs. Ryfka Wagman and her mother were rescued from the ghetto. The Openheimers also survived."

"I remember a large crowd of people on Warsaw Street in the autumn of 1939, among them a group of German soldiers. When I came closer, I saw that the door to a Jewish shop had been smashed and the crowd was pushing inside to loot the store. It was a terrible sight, that Poles should have compromised themselves like that. One person after another shoved his way into that shop. The group of Germans standing there at a distance were laughing hysterically; one of them was taking pictures. I noticed that one of them pointed his finger and said, *'Polnische Schweine, polnische Schweine.'* I got goose bumps all over my body. I stood there for a moment and moved on. I couldn't explain this to myself. Imagine looting like that. Maybe if the store had sugar, bread, flour, chocolate, maybe it wouldn't have made such an impression. But to take iron, chains, pots, spades, buckets. It was an iron goods store."

"Do you remember the Openheimers? That girl was pretty. Esterka."

"The dairy business. They bought milk and cream in every village and sold it to the wholesaler. What else did they control? The shops in the countryside. The Jew sold on credit. He sold cheaper, but he cheated, he added to the bill. They also bought up the right to sell alcohol from the Poles."

"A native of this soil, born in '41. I don't remember the war. But I have often gone to the Rodzińskis', in the neighborhood of the Jewish cemetery, to buy milk. It's a pitiful sight; all those stones that covered the graves have been devastated. Most likely the neighbors took those stones to build their foundations. No one reacted to it."

" 'Jew' is an insult. But I think that certain traditions, certain Jewish customs are very interesting. And if Poles didn't drown themselves in alcohol the way they do, if these same Poles showed more initiative, like the Jews manage to accomplish, then we would have a different reputation in the West. That is why I remember with pleasure the time when I was in the same class with Róża Łaszewska, who later emigrated to Israel.

"I wish that their families' memories would be restored. Whatever that old Poland may have been like, it was their fatherland."

"They say that at a Jewish wedding everyone gets drunk but there's still half a bottle of vodka left over."

"They started communism everywhere, only not in their own country, not in Israel. They were Communists everywhere, only not in their own country. No doubt if Hitler had taken a different position toward them, they would have served Hitler too. In order to preserve their own nation."

"Everyone sympathized with them after the war. It was pitiful. They were so impoverished, so terrorized. But when they started pushing their way into the government, that was a different matter."

"The porter from Mińsk Mazowiecki, Bolek was his name, joined the security organs after the war and persecuted Poles. They shot him in the end. But that's one individual. There were a few such individuals, but one shouldn't judge an entire people on this basis."

"You know the saying 'If you're in need, go see a Jew.' That in itself is proof that there wasn't any anti-Semitism."

"I rented my building supplies warehouse from a Jewish woman; her name was Wagman. She was saved, and her little grandson, daughter, and son-in-law too. She was in the country, out beyond Wyszków, and she pretended to be Catholic. She attended church with her grandson. She had a little prayer book; they marked the book for her so she wouldn't hold it upside down. Her little Andrzej went to church and to confession. He was raised in the Catholic faith. Then they all left for Palestine. Just imagine, Andrzej couldn't get it into his head that his faith was a different faith. And he shot his own grandmother there in Israel. Yes, he shot Mrs. Wagman."

"It was a market day. The trucks were waiting. They transported the old people and the children, and the men and women were forced to walk behind the trucks. Anyone who hung back was shot on the spot. It is hard to revisit those moments in memory."

"Epelbaum was down the street, the brother of that Jew from our building. Then came Jankiel the smith. Next door to him was another smith, Izraelski."

"The tailors went around to people's houses: 'Can I make you a suit, sir?' 'But I don't have any money.' 'I'll do it on credit.'

Then the Jew would come around and collect. He had initiative. Not like Poles. They even sold tea on credit. Ceylon tea. They carried it in tin containers. I haven't drunk such fine tea since the war. A tin of tea cost five zlotys."

"In the Jewish house on the corner there was a huge room with a view of the ghetto. My mother pushed a stroller around it. I watched from that window."

A Hebrew saying defines God as "He who sees without being seen." Was He watching then?

Traces of Mezuzahs

PIASKI, EASTERN POLAND, 1992   When Mr. Świetlicki has time, he shows people like me the traces of mezuzahs on the doorframes of the wooden houses in Piaski. The traces are clear (indentations where the nails were), despite having been covered over many times with oil paint. The traces of memory. Not many people know what a mezuzah is. It is a small parchment scroll containing quotations from the Torah, enclosed in a metal or wooden case, and nailed to the doorframe. It was supposed to remind religious Jews of their faith in God, and at the same time it was a sort of amulet that protected the inhabitants of the house from evil.

What was not destroyed during the war the authorities finished off during the late 1940s and 1950s. There is not a trace left of the synagogue or of the Jewish study houses. A housing development was built on the grounds of one cemetery; a school stands on the grounds of another. That's what people are like. They even took away the sandstone grave markers for whetstones to sharpen knives. Efforts were made to erect a monument and reopen the cemetery or at least to fence in the grounds, but somehow or other they came to nothing, and once again "everything is returning to normal." Two mills are still standing: Weiser's and Hoffman's. "So, are you coming to take them back, miss?"

An old man who dealt in flour with Hoffman remembers him fondly. He says that he sold on credit. He saw them take him away, him and his whole family. They drove them to Trawniki—there was a transit camp there—and then to Bełżec. He says it wasn't so bad with the Jews. One could trade with them. Now it's better, but it wasn't bad then either.

Mogiłkowa Street was the last road of the Jews of Piaski. Before the war they had always been buried with the help of professional mourners. During the occupation the victims were led down the same road. The Germans forbade the Jews to weep.

Mr. Świetlicki's wife was eleven years old when the war broke out. She had been raised with Jews in her father's building. She doesn't remember much, only some fragments. She remembers how they taught her to speak Yiddish; silly things, of course, the way children do. "A neighbor woman came running to my parents to complain about what I said, but I didn't know myself what I'd said."

She remembers a Jewish wedding: how they broke a glass, how they danced, and she was peeking in. That took place in their building. She remembers a red-haired Jewish woman. She doesn't know if she was really red-haired, but she had a red wig. And the teacher from the Jewish school who didn't know how to speak Polish. He taught prayers. And made parchments from skin. "He would stretch the skin on frames, cowskins, I think, and scrape them several times. That was for the holy books. He would scrape them, dry them, and wet them again, I don't know how many times, until they turned into clean parchment." Him she remembers—that Jew.

There were thirty-two children in her class, but only eleven were Catholic; the rest were Jewish. She has photographs; she has counted. She remembers various games. For example, running in front of a Jewish funeral procession. The road to the Jewish cemetery ran in front of the new school. Once the whole class skipped gymnastics and played like that for an hour. The Jews always turned back if you ran across; they would stop, go a few steps back, and return. They could not permit a Gentile to cross in front of a funeral procession.

Mr. Świetlicki collects Jewish souvenirs. Photographs. The Jewish community welcoming the Catholic bishop with bread and salt. They'd also made a welcome gate.

Photographs from the ghetto. "I don't know—maybe some Gestapo officer had gone into the ghetto, selected characteristic individuals, and photographed them. That woman who worked in the photography shop and now lives in Australia simply stole the negatives. And so they were preserved."

Aluminum coins from the ghetto. With a Star of David surrounded by wire.

Jewish melodies and ceremonies.

In addition to the five thousand Piaski Jews, there were several thousand German and Czech Jews in the ghetto. In September 1942 the majority of the Jews from the Piaski ghetto were led out in a column to Trawniki, loaded into freight cars, and transported to Bełżec. The action was carried out by SS men and Ukrainian auxiliary forces. The property left behind by the Jews was placed in bundles and suitcases in the synagogue under the protection of Jewish guards. Those who remained behind were murdered in the Jewish cemetery on a Wednesday in November 1943, in three enormous pits. They had to dig the pits themselves: thirty-three feet long, sixteen wide, and thirteen deep. They undressed completely and were shot. Of course the half alive and the wounded fell in too. More than two thousand people died there.

Eleven-year-old Jakub Kuperblum, using the name Franek Zieliński, lived and worked on Emilia and Adam Kozak's farm in the village of Giełczew near Piaski. He took the cows to graze. He slept in the barn. Once he even tried to hang himself, but the farmer cut him down. People figured out who he was. The boys in the grazing lands wanted to pull down his trousers. He survived until liberation; then he ran away, wrote a letter to Stalin, recalled that he had cousins across the ocean, and left for Canada.

There's a hamlet called Siedliszczki, a mile and a quarter away; a farmer's wife named Aleksandra Pasternak lives there. On his way to Piaski with cabbage, as they tell the story, her husband noticed a bundle wrapped up in a Jewish kerchief, lying in a ditch. He stopped, picked up the year-and-a-half-old child, and returned home. He had two children of his own. "Here," he said to his wife, "we'll raise this one too." The little girl was with the Pasternaks for twenty-two months, until the end of the war. Their neighbors tried to blackmail them, but in vain.

Mrs. Pasternak taught the child prayers and a few words in Polish. She says that she always felt as if someone were watching her, although she saw no one anywhere in the vicinity. Once, when it had been pouring unmercifully for three days in a row, she heard a splashing sound and three men carrying rifles entered her house. "Where is the child?" She showed them the cradle; the child was sleeping. One of the men knelt, kissed the little girl, and said: "We know that you will save the child; please keep on caring for her, and we will repay you." She assumes that they were Jews; there were armed detachments in this area, and he might have been the father.

He survived the war. In July, after the Soviet Army had entered, the mother showed up.

To be precise, they were out in the field when the mother came; someone called for them. But the little girl cried and didn't want to go. The mother came every day for two weeks, day in and day out, caressing and comforting her, and finally the little girl agreed to return to Piaski with her mother and Mrs. Pasternak. When the first Christmas arrived, the first Christmas after liberation, the mother, a Jew, had to get a Christmas tree for the little one because she absolutely wanted a Christmas tree. She also went to church. The little girl was named Johewet; Mrs. Pasternak calls her Basia to this day.

"Her younger sister, Tamara, was abandoned in Bystrzejowice, in the countryside, with a childless family, the Kanclerzes. One morning Mrs. Kanclerz went out to her garden and there was a child wrapped up in a quilt. She thought it was a miracle. Until the end of the occupation they cared for that child as if it were their own. They had happiness in their home. After the war the same family arrived to claim the child, but the Kanclerzes did not want to give her back. They fled west with all their property and the child, to a village far away from all roads. But after a while the child was abducted. Here she is in this photograph, as a young lady. The parents were named Necman. Chana and Lejba. They survived in the Żukowski Forest near Bychawa. Mr. Necman is no longer alive. He was a butcher here in Piaski; now there's a hatter in that building.

"In the village of Brzeziczki near Piaski the Pietrzyk family saved a boy who had run away from the ghetto and whom they found in a field. After the war he left Poland; he lives in Israel.

"In Majdan Jan Ostrowski, a farmer, saved a family of five Jews he knew in a special hiding place in his barn. They were the Chaseks from Piaski. Someone denounced him to the Gestapo; the Jewish family was shot at the entrance to their hiding place on December 24, 1942, and Jan Ostrowski was severely beaten and then transported to the Majdanek concentration camp, where he soon died. The family of Helena and Stanisław Beć from nearby Wyganowice met a similar fate for hiding a Jew."

Someone told Mr. Świetlicki that in 1939 (he was twenty years old then) an officer of the Wehrmacht walked up to him and said, "Jew, get the hell out of Poland as fast as you can because Hitler is going to murder all of you." He rounded up several Jews and his own family and drove to Kowel in a truck. After a while they were deported from there to Siberia. He worked in procurement and survived. After the war he came to Legnica, to a transit camp. And he had an urge to visit Piaski. He went to the station, stood in line for a ticket. But his wife came running up to him and started pleading with him not to go. She wept; she had hysterics: "Don't go; they'll kill you there." He listened to her, left the train, didn't go. That whole group was killed in a pogrom in Kielce in July 1946. "But now," he said, "I had to come. My wife is dead, so I gave myself permission."

"After the war. My deepest regret is that it was already after the war. My wife returned from Auschwitz to her native Radom. She went to a school, and the children there started in: 'What are you doing here, you lousy Jew?' Her uncle, who was in the Polish Army, her uncle, who fought for Poland in a Polish uniform, barely escaped from Poles in Lublin when they recognized him as a Jew.

"Why then, why after the war, why after everything that befell us?"

In Piaski the traces of mezuzahs remain. The mezuzah protected the inhabitants of the house from evil.

⁋‖ Baptism ‖⁋

TOMASZÓW, EASTERN POLAND, 1992   "In 1939 I was in the sixth grade. I was twelve years old. I was a few months shy of thirteen when I was driving a pair of my father's horses to Wożuczyn, eighteen miles from Tomaszów, transporting a wagonload of sugar for wounded soldiers.

"Tomaszów at that time had over ten thousand inhabitants, half of them Jews. The Jews lived in the center of town. You should have seen those little winding streets, narrow, full of mud, filthy. The Jews made a terrible mess on top of that; for example, when they cleaned a chicken, they would throw its guts into the street. I can still see it right in front of my eyes.

"Most of all they worked in trade; they were merchants. They had a beautiful market here, shops, stalls. They were also brokers, middlemen—that is, mainly in the horse trade. I know that whenever my father bought a horse, he absolutely had to pay a broker. What other trades? Tailors, tinsmiths. One was a water carrier. The Tomaszów Jews dressed in the old style and were very religious. They didn't violate their rules. They had a synagogue in Tomaszów, a beautiful big synagogue; it went up in flames during the bombing in September 1939. They also had a Jewish school. They were enormous buildings. Later the Germans blew them up.

"This is how the Jews dressed: black gaberdines, black

suits, yarmulkes. And I never saw a Jew without a beard. The Hasidim had *peyess*. They had the same rights as Poles. There were also Ukrainians in Tomaszów. Those minorities were tolerated very well; it was truly a democracy. For example, in our school—I went to Primary School Number One—there were a lot of Jewish children. Especially in my class. On Saturdays they didn't come to school; they had the day off. There were very few of us students then, and the teachers never introduced a new subject; they only reviewed things, so that the Jewish children wouldn't fall behind. We studied the Roman Catholic religion; we had a priest to teach the catechism. An Orthodox priest came for the Eastern Orthodox children, and Mr. Adler for the Jews. He wasn't dressed Jewish style; he wore an ordinary suit, like gentlemen in offices, elegant. I even had a Jewish teacher in the third and fourth grade: Syla Szpir, a very pretty Jewish woman. Later, in 1939, she worked in a field hospital as a nurse; she took care of the Polish soldiers who were wounded in the battles near Tomaszów. Very competent, very kind. I don't know what happened to her.

"What's inscribed in my memory is a lot of movement in the city. The Jews were always running. For example, late in the afternoon on Friday, when their holy day was about to begin, their Sabbath, a Hasid with *peyess* would run past. When he knocked on a windowpane or a shop door, even if customers were still inside, the Jews would immediately drop everything, and it was the Sabbath. It lasted until sunset on Saturday. During that time they would pray. I have a poem somewhere: 'An old Jew was walking to the synagogue, carrying a thick tome.' I wrote it myself.

"As a child I felt all of that very deeply, even though I didn't much care for Jews at first. In school I simply got dizzy. I ran away from that school. I ran away in the direction of Dąbrowy, on the way to Zamość. People there recognized me and brought me home. I cried, I said the 'Our Father,' and I ran away again. Because that city had an awful effect on me, especially all the movement and those Jews. I didn't have any contact with them; I was very hostile. In the fifth grade I even belonged to an anti-Semitic circle. For example, one day I had an assignment not to allow any Jewish children into class.

"Once, when I was walking to school, I saw people carrying a dead Jew on a stretcher, wrapped up in a sheet. I came to class, and I couldn't focus on the lesson because that image was in front of my eyes the whole time. I wanted to tell the teacher in class what I had seen that day. I raised my hands several times, but she was busy with the lesson. Finally she asked me what was the matter. I was a good student, and the teacher liked me very much. 'I saw them carrying a dropped-dead Jew,' I said. The whole class burst out laughing. The teacher came over to me, stroked my hair, and said, 'Zosia, don't talk like that, they are people too,' and she started speaking very nicely to me on the subject of Jews. I was astonished. How could that be? I had always heard people say 'dropped-dead Jew' on my street. And how, after all, could children behave differently if they saw signs pasted up in the market: 'Down with the Jews!' or 'Don't buy from a Jew!'

"The vice principal of the school was a Mr. Lipkiewicz, who later, during the war, belonged to the Ukrainian partisan gang. He was our teacher for a year. It was he who punished me once by seating me next to a Jewish girl, Topcia. I employed various methods against her; the boys told me what to do, of course. For example, they ordered me to draw a line down the middle of the desk; if she should move her notebook and push it over to my side, I should hit her. She was a nasty little Jew. She would look over at my work and copy everything from me. I had a friend who sat behind me; he would shout, "Beat a Jew with your left hand, because he's not a person." And I did strike her once. I wanted her to go away, not to lean over me. I had a wooden penholder that I gnawed on; I was a nervous child. When I struck her, the veneer peeled off and a piece of it got into her eye. So the little Jewess raised her hand to complain, but the boys threatened her. They yelled that there's going to be one beaten-up Jew. When the teacher wasn't looking, she held her hand up, but when she was looking, she lowered it. So I got away with it.

"When I was in the fourth grade, the priest taught us in religion class how to perform an emergency baptism. He said that anyone can perform a baptism, that the main thing is pouring water over the head. It so happened that the entire school, from first grade to seventh, went in pairs to visit the Tomaszów offices and places of worship. We had only one church then, the larch wood one, and also a synagogue and Orthodox church. The Jews stopped in front of the church because they weren't permitted to go inside. They waited on Church Street while we went inside. In the meantime some boys called me outside and said to me, 'Go tell Topcia that she should come to the vestibule. To the entrance hall.'

" 'Fine,' I said. 'Come, Topcia, you'll see what it's like in our church.' She was afraid. She was religious; in addition to our school, she attended her own Jewish school in the afternoon.

" 'And you won't beat me?' she asked.

" 'Never, just come.'

"So she came along. As soon as she stepped across the threshold, two boys grabbed her and dragged her to the baptismal font. They held her, and I took a handful of holy water and said, 'I baptize you Teresa, in the name of the Father, the Son, and the Holy Spirit.'

"She ran away like someone who has been scalded, screaming and squealing. A huge number of Jews gathered. At first they didn't know what had happened, and then they found out. The boys, who knew what was going on, shouted, 'Zośka, let's run to the ramparts.' They were old defensive ramparts from the seventeenth century. So we fled, far away, beyond the city.

"The next day we didn't go to school. Nor the day after or the day after that. We were afraid; we didn't know how it would end. A Jew, her father, came to the school office, along with a monk from their synagogue, and they demanded that some sort of punishment be meted out. Finally Mr. Sochan, blessed be his memory, a veteran of the Polish Legion and our school custodian, brought my parents a summons to appear in school. There was a hearing in the school office. Mr. Lipkiewicz walked around me with a yardstick and wanted me to hold out my hand and apologize to that little Jewess and also apologize to her father. Of course I didn't want to; the boys had told me to clasp my hands tightly so that no one could pull them apart. I faithfully upheld the agreement that had arisen from our anti-Semitic conspiracy. It went on for a long time. The principal of the school, as I can see now, acted very kindly, very wisely; she wanted to soften me, to turn me into a human being, but I resisted and stuck with the boys. In the end as a punishment they made us stand under the staircase during recess, as the guilty ones. That's how I made up for that. And I changed completely in my attitude toward Topcia. I no longer persecuted her; I considered her a Christian now. That cured me completely.

"Afterward, the next year and throughout all the years until the war broke out, I liked one Jewish girl very much, Esterka Cytryn. She lived right here. There was a fenced-off Jewish lumberyard here; her father owned it. We were great friends. After that baptism it seems I changed a great deal.

"I remember that later on I met that poor Jewish girl Topcia Becker in the street, the one I had christened Teresa. It was when the general liquidation of the Jews had begun. They herded them into the lumberyard. When I remember that now, I am ashamed for us, for us Poles. Oh, what it looked like: They herded the Jews into the yard, and if people didn't come on their own, they searched for them from building to building and shot them, killed them on the spot. And people were already driving in from the villages in their sleds, there was snow on the ground, and they took whatever they could from the Jewish houses. Junk, worthless things, pots and pans. The Jews were poor by then, worn down; there were only bedbugs and hunger in those houses. Bełżec was already in operation. Only they didn't take them there directly from Tomaszów, but via Cieszanów, and from there to Bełżec. It was horrendous, that day, when they shot them, shot even the sick who were lying on their quilts. And I saw Topcia standing among the sleds that were parked there. Suddenly she emerged from among the sleds, wearing a black kerchief tied in back of her head, and then she drew back. She was terrified. I gave her some bread and said to her, 'Teresa, don't worry, you have been baptized.' She didn't say anything; she just looked at me. I have the impression that at first she was afraid that I would denounce her. But I was no longer the same person.

"During the war a young Jewish boy, he was maybe twenty years old, used our grindstones to grind grain that he brought in his pockets. He had two old, sickly parents. He got the rye from somewhere and begged my father to let him grind it. Father allowed him to do it, but you could hear it on the road, so I would stand in the yard with a hoe as if I were working, and when someone walked by, I would thump, and the Jew would stop so no one would hear because they would take us too to a camp for that. The day the Germans drove the Jews into that lumberyard was a Wednesday, I remember, a nice March day, quite warm, but the snow was deep. I had been in town in the morning, and I was returning home along the street that they were walking on to that yard. I saw gendarmes, five of them, slender, wearing the finest brown gloves, elegantly dressed, their boots gleaming. And the Jews seemed to be feverish. They had to get to the place themselves. It so happened that some of them were already in the yard, but they went back to get something else; they darted in and out, walked, ran; they didn't know what to do with themselves. An elderly Jew with a beard was walking along. He had on his Jewish armband, and the Jews had orders that when they passed a German, they had to bow. And this poor little Jew, he was frozen; I think he was also hungry, because he looked so poor, but despite this, there was something noble in that figure. They are a chosen people; you have to take that into account. And that Jew did bow, but the German lashed him so hard across the face with a riding crop with a lead ball at the tip, that he knocked his eyeball out. The Jew controlled himself, ooooh, that's all he whispered ever so softly, the blood spurted out of him, and he ran off. And the German looked at me provocatively and burst out laughing, ha-ha-ha. Maybe he thought I was a *Volksdeutsch*? I was wearing a brown coat that my sister, who had been shipped to Germany, sent me, because we had nothing to wear.

"And in the yard, my God, what went on there later. The Germans kept shooting, and the townspeople of Tomaszów were already waiting on the corner with sleds, with horses; even my father was appointed to transport those Jews. To Cieszanów, I think; that's what I heard. It went on for a long time, from ten o'clock to three in the afternoon. They segregated them in the yard; they directed the young Jews into columns and onto a truck. I have a photograph of the Germans leading them down the forest road to Bełżec. There were many dead people lying in and around the houses. But for some reason, maybe deliberately, a Jewish carter had been kept alive; his business had been delivering goods to the stores—flour from the mill, for example. He owned his own sled and a skinny white horse, all of them barely alive. I remember, right on that street over there, near the station, there were narrow little streets, wooden houses, the oldest section of the city; all of it burned down, and what's there now is new. So, entire stacks of Jews lay across those sleds—men, women, children, murdered in their homes. Whoever didn't go to the yard—they went into their houses, and if they found them, they killed them. And they ordered that Jew to transport them. Then he too perished, because all the Jews in Tomaszów perished. Every last one of them.

"Even much later, in October, when Mama and I were going to early mass, I saw a German chasing two Jewish women, pale, from over there beyond the church, I don't know where they had been hiding, maybe in some pits. One of them had a tiny girl with her; she must have been about three years old. He was taking them to be killed. One of my schoolmates, Miss Lederkremer, a pretty Jewish girl, worked in the German police warehouse. She was with the Germans for a long time, but then they killed her too. They used her, and not just for work. At times I would see her riding through town; she was smiling. Maybe even then she had enough to eat, or maybe she hoped they would leave her alone. But they killed her. Sometimes, when you were sitting in the house, you could hear shots in the street. And then, in that Bełżec, that column of fire.

"I slept at my father's place. We were in hiding. There were three sisters still at home (I was the youngest of the sisters) and also two brothers. We were in the conspiracy; the partisans would come to us; I am a member of the World Union of Soldiers of the Home Army, with the rank of sergeant. We hid in the attic; Father would cover us up with straw and sheaves of wheat. The attic window faced south. You could see that terrifying column of fire from Bełżec. It seemed as if the sky were burning. At night there was a red glow. Of course we saw it! In the beginning people didn't know very much about it because they didn't burn them; they just put them to death in the gas chambers and placed them in huge mass pits that were more than three hundred feet long, sixty-five feet wide, and forty deep. Facedown, facing the earth, the bottom. One on top of the other. And when they had piled up a big enough mound . . . I know this from Dr. Peter, with whom I worked in the museum afterward; he was the hospital director at that time. Dr. Peter himself told me, because he had contacts, even with someone from the Bełżec camp, thanks to whom there are those photographs in the museum. When they built up a pile like that, then they covered it over with earth and waited until . . . The remains swell for a couple of days; they produce gas; the grave swells and then sinks down again. But even that didn't help them, even though they used ten layers of earth. Because what happened was, when the hot weather set in in summer, streams of plasma started flowing out of there, pus from those rotting bodies. They poured concrete over it, but it broke open. Then they brought in an excavator and flatbed trucks and loaded the remains they unearthed onto them. It produced a disgusting stench.

"You know where Bełżec was and where we were, and we could not sit near an open window in the summer and eat our supper, because it stank terribly of corpses outside the window from that Bełżec. I couldn't look at it anymore; I had some kind of dementia. I couldn't understand why that was going on, the burning and burning. During quiet days, before it rained, you could even hear the railroad from Bełżec when a train came in, and then you could also hear the music. Because they played music at night. At night they didn't put people to death. But Jews selected from the transports had to play right next to the pits. What did they play? They played whatever they were told to play.

"As for that excavator, when it dug them out of the ground, many an inhabitant of Bełżec could see what was going on: an arm, a leg hanging from that excavator's shovel. And bodies that were only partially decomposed. A death mill. One Jew from Lwów, Reder, he was an educated Jew, a chemist, the owner of a soap factory, he managed to escape. They brought him to Bełżec, but since he looked fine, healthy, they left him alive; they always let five hundred live, the so-called gravediggers, to bury those who were murdered. If one of them grew weak while he was working, they would push him into the pit and get the next one. A woman hid Reder in town, where he'd gone with two gendarmes. One of them went off somewhere; the other dozed off. That's how he escaped. The woman cooked for a German dog, so she stole meat and fed that Jew. He survived.

"I think that the majority acted properly. But there were hyenas too. Not necessarily Poles; they came from the various minorities around here. There were also instances of people hiding them. You have to take one thing into consideration: that if someone denounced you, if the Germans found out, then your entire family would perish. There were two barns near us, and it was obvious that Jews were hiding there, but there were people who went there with bayonets and shouted, 'Crawl out, Jew, crawl out, Jew.' And led them away. I know many of the farmers' stories. I was in contact with Jeziorna and other villages; a Mr. Cabko there told me who was hiding Jews and who led an entire family into the forest and killed them all. There are all sorts of stories. I, for one, cannot imagine how it was possible to shelter a Jew. When we allowed one to grind grain, Father was absolutely terrified. But I have to say that very few people denounced them. Today you can't tell anyone anything in confidence, but then people knew what was going on in other people's homes. One farmer told me how he sheltered a Jew: He made him a hiding place in the barn; he built a doghouse in the barn, and it looked as if he were bringing food to the dog, but actually he was giving it to the Jew. People tried different things. In Bełżec the priest's mother hid a Jewish woman and her daughter while she had a German officer quartered in her house.

"On the fiftieth anniversary of the outbreak of the war I went to the school that I attended in 1939. I walked into my old classroom and told the teachers not to bother me, that I wanted to be alone. I sat at the desk and began to read out the names. I have a list, all the names that I have remembered, so many years, but I shut my eyes, and I saw where each one sat. And I read out their names. Present, absent—I made a mark. Topcia Becker, Toba Engelsztein, Ryfka Borg, Dworcia Szmuc, Chajka Pancer, Mindla Goldman—she was such a delicate Jewish girl. Sajkiewicz, also a Jewess, I don't remember her first name. Taubenblatt, Tepler. My blond Esterka. Killed. Dead, dead, dead."

⊰| CEMETERIES |⊱

EASTERN POLAND, 1993   He didn't have the strength to go to Poland. "For me, Poland is a cemetery of the Jewish people. I couldn't bear that journey into the valley of human tragedy. Everything that was once my life is today dead and buried. I write about what was, and I know where I am."

The Wandering Jew traveled the world with his humpback for his house. For many hundreds of years he found shelter in the land full of forests. *"Po-lin,* here you will rest," a voice said to him from heaven. "Here you will spend the night."

At the time he did not appreciate the tragedy of that metaphor.

Cemeteries. In Hebrew—houses of tombs, houses of life, houses of eternity. In Yiddish—a good place, a holy place.

A knot, an ornament encircling the epitaph. May his (her) soul be tied in the knot of life.

"For I know that my redeemer lives, and on the last day I shall rise from the earth. To the blessed memory of my dearest parents Miriam and Mendele Griner, my sisters Szajnda and Sura, and all the murdered Jews, we who are grateful to God for our salvation . . ."

Those who survived the war stubbornly repeat, like Joseph Shapiro from *The Penitent*, "Where was He when the Jews of Poland dug their own graves? Where was He when the Nazis played with the skulls of Jewish children? If He does exist and He kept silent, He is as much a murderer as Hitler. . . ."

The graves are overgrown with grass. Like memory. The cemeteries are overgrown with grass. The Jewish cemeteries in Poland become overgrown more quickly, more easily, more thoroughly than anywhere else. The headstones are covered with moss, grass, and weeds. They sink into the earth. They return to the earth. Irena, who spends whole days at Jewish cemeteries, says it's better that way; at least they won't be destroyed. Their place is there, in the belly of the earth.

Stone monuments, "lapidariums." Now they are erecting "lapidariums." Walls of memory made of fragments, remnants set in cement.

Cemeteries of memory. In the little town of Kazimierz on the Vistula River I used to play as a child on a big hill, unaware that I was playing in the Jewish cemetery. There were remnants there still, gravestones of Polish sandstone, that had grown into the earth. They used to call it weeping stone.

Every shortcut in an old Jewish town today goes through a burial ground (the *kirkut*, the Jewish cemetery). A woman who lives in Szczebrzeszyn right beside the cemetery, which is overgrown with nettles and head-high weeds, says, "I am not afraid of ghosts, and I have dogs to protect me from people. It's overgrown here because no one important is buried here, no *zaddik*, and who's going to bother about simple tailors and watchmakers? No one remembers them. Only the trees say prayers. But do they know the Kaddish?"

From the Tomaszów chronicle of one Jan Mazurek:

In Tomaszów since the founding of the city there existed a Jewish cemetery called the *kirkut* or *okopisko*. The Germans destroyed it while the Jews were still alive—i.e., in 1942–43. The destruction began with removing the limestone gravestones and boulders, which were used to pave the muddiest streets. Those stones are still there today on Rymarska and Starozamojska streets, their inscriptions facedown on the earth, and there are a great many of them. They were used to make a sidewalk around the house of the German district supervisor. At present in the old cemetery there are neither monuments nor trees, which the Germans cut down for fuel. The cemetery's walls were taken apart by the inhabitants since they contained good, though old, bricks.

Today only the old people can say what a Jewish funeral procession looked like. A Jew, when he died, lay in his house in a specially darkened room without any lights—that is, without candles; only a small kerosene lamp burned at his head. After the deceased was washed, he was wrapped in a sheet and placed on a bier, a kind of stretcher lashed together with straps, without any nails, two long and two short poles and two boards in between. Four Jews, specially hired for this service, carried the bier; behind them walked the family and one or two professional mourners, depending on the wealth of the deceased. The rabbi did not walk with the funeral procession; only one of their elders did, someone like our church organist, who sang very rapidly as he walked, and in general the entire procession walked to the cemetery in great haste, as if they were in a hurry to do the burying. The grave was dug like a normal grave, but the corpse was placed in a sitting rather than a prone position, with the face toward the rising sun. People said that they placed a shard of pottery on the dead man's eye and buried him like that, so as not to get earth in his eyes. A Jewish funeral procession didn't differ at all from funerals in ancient times. If a Jew's wife died, he had to sit at home in mourning for fourteen days, eating once a day and not moving. He was not even permitted to lie down to sleep.

The Tomaszów cemetery holds several generations of Jews who were buried there over three centuries. Only the last Jews were not fated to rest in it since they perished in the death camps of Bełżec, Sobibór, and Majdanek.

At present the area is uncared for, not fenced in. Cows graze here, and if someone does not know that this was once a Jewish cemetery, he would never recognize it as such. No, there are no longer any Jews in Tomaszów today. True, two remain, but they are converts. One is a very good Catholic who goes to confession and is decent and pious; no one would recognize him as a former Jew. The other is neither a Jew nor a Catholic, even though he was baptized.

The rest of the Tomaszów Jews, who survived in Russia, returned after the war, but not to Tomaszów—to Wrocław, Kluczbork, Wałbrzych. They don't even show their faces here in order not to add to their grief. They are trying to emigrate to America or Palestine because as they themselves say, they have nothing in Poland but sorrowful memories. Their property that survived the war they sold through a Jew to whom they gave power of attorney to deal with these matters; his name was Szymon. A very decent little Jew; he survived the occupation in one of the nearby villages, hiding with a peasant. The Jewish cemeteries in Tyszowce, Łaszczów, and Komorów, as well as Jarczów, met the same fate as the one in Tomaszów: There is almost no trace of them.

The last Singer demon lived in the town of Tyszowce. The town was a godforsaken hole, forgotten by both the Lord and people. The last demon lived on Jewish books that had survived the catastrophe. He was the last of the tempters. Naturally he was a Jew, although apparently Gentile demons also existed. He was the last because who needs demons if man himself is a demon?

Andrzej and Irena are in the sixteenth-century Jewish synagogue in Lublin. They are photographing gravestones. They show me stones that are shattered, smashed, once again nonexistent. The grave of a *zaddik;* three other important graves. A mound overgrown with weeds, nettles, grass, and wildflowers. The *zaddik*'s grave looks black beside a large number of slips of paper, many of them torn, with Hebrew and Yiddish petitions. Wind. The scraps, shreds, ashes of letters flutter in the wind. I cannot understand them. Suddenly a large man, with a beard and *peyess,* enters this frame, dressed in a gaberdine and a hat; he climbs up and stops beside the *zaddik*'s grave. He has come from New York. Swaying rhythmically, he prays from a large leather-bound prayer book with gold letters on the spine.

During my trip back to Warsaw from Lublin a young man in the train chews me out for reading a book by that disgusting Jew Singer. Don't we have enough real Polish writers?

When I tell Professor R. about this, he says one has to admit that some people are crazy but that this is not a purely Polish trait, as is commonly thought. However, it does occur. The professor is, as always, full of exalted equanimity. But even he admits that a Jewish cemetery is not the safest place in the world for a woman on her own. "You should take a bodyguard and Mace."

To describe something missing, the shape of absence. Images, tastes, remnants, fragments, memories, grains of memories. A patchwork made of other people's memories; everyone contributes something: a chunk, a piece of glass, a grain, a pebble. Not only the truth about them, not only their image but mine too, my country's, what it could have been if they were there too. The graves are becoming overgrown, and the last demons feeding on Jewish manuscripts are beginning to die of hunger in Poland.

⢻ I Am Not a Racist ⡇

Polish children know very little about Jews. In the spring of 1990 I administered a questionnaire on this subject in the Warsaw schools. More than two hundred students, ages ten to fifteen, participated.

Forty-five percent of the children (the youngest) know nothing about Jews. ("I don't know anything, so I have no opinion.") The rest describe them with misspelled labels: "a historycle Israllite people"; "they speak Hibbrew." The majority write about injustices done to the Jews during the Second World War: "murdered, beaten, condemned, destroyed, persecuted, hated by the Germans. . . ."

The twelve-year-olds know more about the wartime tragedy of the Jewish people. But they already voice biting comments about "Jewish greed." Eight out of thirty-eight have decidedly unfavorable opinions. In the ninth grade, one quarter do. The Jews are accused of communism and of controlling the Polish people. A remark about the regime, which they supposedly control, with a strong emphasis on Polish suffering and a characteristic sense of superiority, is repeated five times. But among the eighth and eleventh graders there are also opinions condemning anti-Semitism ("it is an incomprehensible thing") and lengthy statements that are a kind of justification of their own tolerance ("that is why I think that they are just the same as other people and we shouldn't treat them differently").

The opinions become more radical among the older children. In addition to a greater fund of information, they are characterized by a striking self-confidence. There is an increase in their feeling of national identity, in the worst possible meaning of this term. Anti-Semitism appears in the form of unconcealed loathing and an attitude of domination based on superiority (racial, moral, in general). This occurs even in opinions that are supposedly positive or in fragments that graciously call upon others to accept equal rights. "I am not a racist, but . . ." There is a clear division between the defenders of "the other" and those who absolutely reject them. Jews are "cunning," "shrewd," "have a head for business." They are usually "swindlers."

"During the war Jews had a lot of trouble because the Germans murdered them, tore their skin off and made shoes out of it."—M., ten years old.

"I like the Jews; they know how to run a business."—K., ten years old.

"Jews are very intelligent, and that's why the Germans hated them and shot them."—G. B., ten years old.

"Jews: murdered, cunning, cheaters."—G., ten years old.

"The Jews are a nomadic people. They are one of the oldest peoples. Now they are fighting in Palestine for their own people, but they are murdering Arabs for no reason at all."—K., ten years old.

"The Jews are a tribe that I don't like. Hitler didn't like the Jews because he murdered them, but he had a Jewish mistress. The Jews are a plague."—T., ten years old.

"The Germans murdered the Jews in Treblinka and made ashes out of them."—R., ten years old.

"As for the Jews, it was because of them that we had a war, because they were hiding in Poland."—A., ten years old.

"The Jewish people during the war were murdered by the German Democratic Republic. They are a wealthy people, and they don't believe in God. During the war the Jews swallowed gold to keep the Germans from appropriating their riches."—K., ten years old.

"The Jews live among us."—B., ten years old.

"Many famous people are descended from the Jews."—B. R., ten years old.

"I always associate Jews with long beards. It seems to me that they are a people who are scattered over the whole world, but the majority of them live in Poland."—P., ten years old.

"I think that you have to feel sorry for the Jews because of what they suffered during the war. They are good and decent, but I don't like them."—M., ten years old.

"The Jews are old people, old people who always had bad luck. They were always persecuted. There is a Jewish cemetery in Warsaw."—N., eleven years old.

"The Jews, in my opinion, are deceitful and cunning. A lot of people don't like Jews."—Y., eleven years old.

"The Jews' fatherland is Israel. But they are distributed throughout the whole world. In Poland before the war there were as many as 3.5 million of them. Jews are naturally talented at business. That is why many of them are in trade. Poles are proud that they expelled most of the Jews in 1968. I think that Jews are a clever people. The names of many famous people testify to this—for example, Einstein."—U., eleven years old.

"Before the war there were a lot of them in Poland. During the war the Germans murdered many of them. In our times they are less visible, but apparently several individuals in the government are Jews. Jews are very talkative. They are good at buying and selling."—Z., eleven years old.

"I think that now, after those terrible years, we ought to treat them like people."—J., twelve years old.

"I think about the Jews, in fact I am almost sure, that they are people just like us. I believe that their different nationality, language, and speech do not distinguish them from normal people."—K., twelve years old.

"The Jews are the least happy people on earth. They don't have their own state, and during the war, 'thanks' to Hitler's crimes, they were eradicated to a great extent."—M., twelve years old.

"The Jews introduced communism into Poland. During the war they were very persecuted by the Germans. Poles hid them in their homes, risking their own lives. For what we did for them they haven't shown enough gratitude. They took a lot of things from Poland. Then they occupied high positions."—L. B., twelve years old.

"The Jews took complete control of our country. In the government they are all Jews. I wouldn't have anything against their living in Poland, but I am extremely opposed to their ruling our country."—A., fourteen years old.

"Jews are a people who are known for trickery and cheating in their own interest. The one virtue of Jews is their ability to 'make' money. In my opinion, we have Jews in our government."—SOS, fourteen years old.

"I will never forgive Solidarity for putting Poland in the hands of the Jewish minority."—XYZ, fourteen years old.

Soon these children will no longer be children.

There are no official statistics. The Social-Cultural Society of Polish Jews has barely three thousand members. An American organization, the Joint Distribution Committee, estimates the number of Jews in Poland as around ten thousand. For every Jew, then, we have three Esperantists, twelve Jehovah's Witnesses, fifteen members of the Union of Philatelists. There are two thirds of a million adherents of the Eastern Orthodox faith. Among the minorities in Poland the Jews are in a very distant last place.

Not everyone knows this. According to polls that have been taken, 1 in 4 Poles is convinced that from 350,000 to 3.5 million Jews are living in Poland. One in 10 believes that there are significantly more, perhaps 4 million, perhaps as many as 7 million.

PART THREE

There

⫷| Two Suitcases |⫸

If necessary, the whole world can fit into two suitcases. A few clothes and some manuscripts. Hobgoblins and demons traveled without baggage.

Isaac Bashevis Singer left Poland on April 19, 1935. Like countless East European Jews before and after him, he was traveling to the promised land, to America. He had only a tourist visa in his passport, obtained for him by his brother, but he knew that he would not return to Poland. Like Aaron from *Shosha*, he yearned to leave that land at any price; the dark specter of nazism was already hanging over Europe. Traveling to the West, he looked out at Germany from his train window; the Germans were celebrating Hitler's forty-sixth birthday at the time. He was in a hurry. He turned down an opportunity to wait for the luxury liner *Normandie* in order to escape as soon as possible from a world that was beginning to choke him.

He was the third of the four Singer siblings to leave Poland. The eldest, his sister Hindele Esther, had left first, shortly before the outbreak of World War I. She was temperamental and suffered from nerves, having been kept in a cradle under a table by her wet nurse. Within the family she was called a Hasid in skirts, and she struggled throughout her life with the verdict of the Jewish religion that condemned a woman to being a "nobody." She envied her brothers their privileged position, the possibility of acquiring learning, studying the Torah and Talmud, and she rebelled against the role that fate had assigned her. In her brother's literary portraits she is often in the power of a dybbuk.

Bashevis noted that the first signs of literary talent with the Singer family showed up in Hindele Esther's letters to her fiancé. They were lost, like her early literary essays, which she destroyed, following her mother's advice, while crossing the Polish border by train in 1914.

She was married off to Abraham Kreitman, a diamond cutter from Antwerp with whom she moved to England. The marriage was not successful. In 1926 Hindele Esther returned to Poland for a visit with her son. She spent the summer with her two brothers in Świder, a minor resort near Warsaw, in the house of the poet Alfred Kacyzne, among the elite of Jewish writers. When she returned to London three months later, she started writing.

Her autobiographical *Dance of Demons* appeared in Yiddish in Warsaw in 1936 and ten years later in London in English translation, under the title *Deborah*. She was the first in Singer's family to reach for a pen in order to describe their common childhood and youth. When her book appeared, she was forty-five years old. Joshua already had the success of *Yoshe Kalb* behind him, and Isaac Bashevis had published *Satan in Goray*. Hindele Esther transformed her own autobiography into a fictional story with a third-person narrator, designed to distance herself from the painful past. Unlike her brothers, who scrupulously and nostalgically re-created their early years in their memoirs, she wanted to liberate herself from the hold of that time.

Deborah was moderately successful, and Hindele Esther,

under the name of Esther Kreitman, continued her literary endeavors as a translator into Yiddish, translating Dickens and Shaw. She also wrote another novel and a collection of short stories. She spent her life in London and died there in 1954 at the age of sixty-three.

After the departure of Isaac Bashevis, only the youngest son, Moshe, remained in Poland. By then he was living in the small town of Stary Dzików in eastern Poland, where he had moved with his parents in the early 1920s. Pinchas Singer had obtained a rabbinical post there. Moshe, a Hasid possessed, his *peyess* dangling to his shoulders, was called a saint. Indifferent to the world, in a floor-length gaberdine, a shirt without buttons, and old-fashioned shoes, he prayed and sang constantly, clapping his hands. Like other devout Hasidim, he would fall into religious ecstasy. He continued living with his mother after Pinchas Singer died in 1929 at the age of sixty-one.

After the outbreak of World War II Moshe and his mother were deported to Soviet Central Asia, sharing the fate of hundreds of thousands of Poles and Polish Jews. Shipped in cattle cars, they got as far as Kazakhstan. Unloaded in the empty steppe in the middle of the winter, they were ordered to build their own shelter from whatever scraps could be found. Famine, misery, and the brutal conditions in the war-torn Soviet Union did not weaken Moshe's faith. Maurice Carr, Hindele Esther's son, relates the testimony of someone who shared the Singers' fate: Starved and weakened, Moshe still refused to eat a piece of bread he was offered one *Shabbas*, afraid that it might not be kosher.

Toward the end of the war three postcards from Dzhambul, a city in Kazakhstan, arrived at Hindele Esther's London address. There was no fourth card. No information exists about the fate of Isaac Bashevis Singer's mother and his youngest brother.

On May 1, 1935, along with the other passengers traveling tourist class on the French ship *Champlain,* among them a Pearl Liebgott from the Polish town of Częstochowa and a Frieda Schwartz from Romania, Isaac ended his voyage on Ellis Island. The American immigration officer anglicized his name from the Polish Zynger. After assuring the officer that he was neither a polygamist nor an anarchist, he received an entry stamp in his passport.

His America began in Sea Gate in Coney Island, where his brother was spending the summer. He was greeted there by jazz music, a noisily whirling Ferris wheel, and a black-skinned giant with two dwarfs on his shoulders. That colorful, tumultuous world, full of unusual people, was so far removed from his familiar Hasidic heaven and hell as to seem unreal. What he missed most of all was Jewish spirits and demons.

In his autobiography he analyzes that state of early emigration several times: "I had cut off whatever roots I had in Poland and yet I knew that I would remain a stranger here to my last day. . . . Nothing was left for me in the future. All I could think about was the past. My mind returned to Warsaw, to Świder, to Stefa's apartment on Niecała Street, to Esther's furnished room on Świętojerska. I again had to tell myself that I was a corpse."

Sea Gate was the center of Yiddish culture in New York. His brother's home was frequented by famous guests—writers, critics, journalists, and actors. Israel Joshua Singer's popularity in America was equivalent to Sholem Asch's. Both were recognized as outstanding prose writers of Yiddish literature. Surrounded with respect and recognition, Joshua had continued his career on the other side of the ocean. Right after his arrival he had begun publishing his great novel *The Brothers Ashkenazi* in the Yiddish daily *Forward*. It had been successfully adapted for the stage, just like his next saga, *The Family Carnovsky*.

There were frequent discussions in Sea Gate about literature and politics. The atmosphere was similar to Warsaw's. And just as in Warsaw, Isaac Bashevis was referred to as Singer's younger brother.

Dressed in a light American suit and a soft-collared shirt, he had to admit that his black hat, his vest, and his wide suspenders were relics of the past. Changing his inner dress would prove to be much more difficult, perhaps even impossible.

It seemed to him that the Yiddish language and literature written in that language had no chance of a future, yet he did not abandon his literary efforts in the language of his demons. For a long time he complained about an inability to write, but almost from the beginning he placed pieces in the *Forward*. Soon he was to publish installments of his first novel, *The Sinful Messiah,* a fictionalized biography of Jacob Frank, the eighteenth-century false prophet. The newspaper became his literary home, and his collaboration with the *Forward* continued almost to the end of his life.

He spent a great deal of time in cafeterias, those self-service restaurants where he met other émigrés from Eastern Europe like himself. Everything there was familiar: the food, the words, the mood. He almost was able to touch the past. Not like in the streets of multilingual, theatrical, raucous Manhattan.

He thought that his departure from Poland was the greatest mistake of his life. A feeling of degradation and humiliation never left him. For a long time he did not know who he was. He was taking his first steps. On paper too.

In 1937, two years after he came to America, Singer spent his summer in Mountaindale, in the Catskills. He stayed at an inexpensive boardinghouse, which reminded him of the summer pensions in Poland, where he used to listen for hours to the heated discussions among Jewish intellectuals. Here too he was surrounded by Jews, many of them recent immigrants from Europe.

During that summer he met Alma Haimann, a German Jew from a solid middle-class background, a married mother of two children. She too had left Europe in 1935. Well educated, with an interest in literature, she was impressed with the young, shy writer, who seemed in dire need of motherly care. Like most assimilated German Jews, Alma did not speak Yiddish. The two recent émigrés communicated in English, taking long walks and spending afternoons on the veranda.

They continued seeing each other in New York. Two years later Alma Haimann left her family and moved in with Isaac. They were married in February 1940, and she took a job as a salesclerk in a department store. It was to be Singer's only marriage, a childless one; they were together for more than fifty years. Alma Singer never learned Yiddish and never read any of her husband's books in the language in which they were created.

In February 1944 Israel Joshua Singer died suddenly of a heart attack in his New York apartment. He was fifty-one years old. The previous evening he and his brother had eaten supper together. Isaac called the death the greatest calamity of his life.

He was alone. Although no one at that time could fully comprehend the almost total annihilation of East European Jews, the universe he knew as his own was gone forever. Other than Alma, he had nobody he could call a close friend. He was living with her in Manhattan, near Central Park, on a continent distant from the war, far away from Stalin and Hitler. In his night table drawer lay his passport with a valid visa. In time he was to make this new world his own. Yet within his inner self he remained a perennial refugee, never able to abandon the two suitcases he had brought with him from Poland.

THE LAST ONE

NEW YORK, 1992   Samuel L. Shneiderman began writing poetry when he was twelve years old. He wrote in both Yiddish and Polish. Then he translated the Polish poets Kazimierz Wierzyński and Władysław Broniewski into Yiddish and also Jankiel's entire concert from *Pan Tadeusz*, the great Polish Romantic poem. He was a friend of avant-garde poets Adam Ważyk, Anatol Stern, Aleksander Wat. In the twenties he worked for the *Literarishe bleter*, the Yiddish equivalent of the Polish-language *Literary News*. It published stories, poetry, theater reviews, interviews with writers, and articles about them. He remembers that place and the Writers' Club as the center of literary life for prewar Jewish Warsaw. That's where he first met Isaac Bashevis Singer.

"Bashevis worked as a proofreader and wrote stories at the same time. People would come out of the editorial office, grab his hand, extract a piece for the next day. 'Wait, wait,' he'd say, 'I'm almost finished.' He didn't attach much importance to this. But he was exceptionally gifted; it came very easily to him. Apparently he produced his novels in installments; afterward they called it great literature. Isn't that right? American popular novels are probably worse; at least every so often Singer would throw in some pictures from real life. Sometimes his texts would be sent back, the journalistic ones; he made up a lot, he simply invented things; they didn't trust his facts.

"He was very thin then; he had fiery red hair and a Machiavellian gaze. He used to sit in the Writers' Club next to the one heated wall; he was always freezing. He often made jokes, mimicked his colleagues; a particularly successful imitation was of one of the critics who liked to tell anecdotes. He would also go downstairs to the printshop. The printers were two brothers who especially amused Bashevis. He even wrote a story about them. He had a sense of humor, but he was basically a very serious person. He was knowledgeable about many things; he knew a great deal. A mystic, but a mystic plagued by doubts. Very well read, but there are no apparent influences in his writing.

"He was ugly. He mocked everyone. A cynic, but a wise cynic. A very gifted storyteller. He didn't recognize any taboos in his writing; he violated the taboos of Yiddish literature. No, I never imagined when I knew him in Warsaw that he would be a Nobel laureate. Never. In those days he was considered the younger brother of Israel Joshua.

"He looked like a hermit, but a hermit who was consumed by a thirst for life and passion for women, love of travel and of seeing the world."

Shneiderman was born in Kazimierz on the Vistula. His house still stands there.

"My father wore a gaberdine, but I walked around in Kazimierz without a hat. In the twenties, I remember, the neighbors came to my father to complain. But he sent them away, saying, 'It's none of your business; let him do what he wants to do.' We lived in an apartment building on the market square. In Kazimierz there wasn't the same fear that existed in other small towns. For example, when a church procession passed, Jews would lock themselves up and hide, but not in Kazimierz. We even attended Catholic weddings. That would not have been possible anywhere else. I know that the priest in Kazimierz used to visit my father, who was a superb Talmud scholar, and debate religion with him—in Polish; my father spoke excellent Polish. At home my parents spoke Yiddish with each other. But the children spoke Polish. I remember that when Jerzy Kuncewicz, who was a lawyer married to a famous writer, came to see my father, he was astonished when he heard how well he spoke Polish. In fact there were many such Jews in Kazimierz. My grandfather, who was the unofficial architect of Kazimierz, knew even more Polish sayings. He was exceptionally talented. He could read Hebrew, Yiddish, Polish, and French.

"Father dealt in leather; he also had a factory that produced boot uppers.

"Kazimierz was the one town where Jewish writers who wrote in Yiddish associated with Polish writers. I wouldn't call it integration, but they did get together. Asch wrote his famous book *The Shtetl* about Kazimierz. It is romantic, idealized, but it all takes place in the landscape of Kazimierz. Stanisław Witkiewicz used to visit there. He became friends with Sholem Asch, even though Asch spoke Polish very poorly. Witkiewicz asked Asch why he didn't write in Polish. 'How can I write in Polish when the Vistula speaks to me in Yiddish?' he answered.

"Singer was a master of the Yiddish language. His style, that style of his, is envied by so many Yiddish writers. What a style! And what a storyteller! He had an exceptional mastery of the language, which is why no translation can possibly convey it. He was steeped in Jewishness from his earliest years. He lived in one of those little towns, Radzymin, that were the source of the Yiddish language. He knew all its colors and shapes. He was a very wise, very intelligent man, but cynical.

Oh, was he cynical! He used to laugh at the Yiddish avant-garde in the most awful way, even though he himself published in their journals. And the avant-gardists envied him his roots, which they did not have.

"He may have visited Kazimierz once, as I recall, but he wasn't interested in it; for him, Kazimierz was colored, false, inauthentic. Was it really like that? Yes, absolutely. Those weren't the simple, provincial Jews that he knew. They were more polished, more educated; put simply, it was different milieu. Also artists, intellectuals, and with Polish connections as well; it was different, more refined.

"I think that *Satan in Goray* is a fascinating book, perhaps the best of all the books he wrote. There is a whole primitive literature on the subject of devils, dybbuks, and so forth. It is not even considered literature. Little brochures sold in synagogues. Popular, penny-press histories of satanic figures, of Jewish life. Do you know what is the top Jewish bestseller of the last four hundred years? It is the *Pentateuch for Women,* biblical stories told in a simple language, a colorful reworking for women. It was called *Tsene Urene*—'Let's go out and see.' Let us go out from our tightly circumscribed life and see the world. Rabbi Isaac Rabin of Janów in Lublin Province began its publication. In the synagogues the men read from the Old Testament, and the women from that translated Bible. Bashevis collected such literature; he thought of it as a source.

"But he had no desire to cooperate, to create something in a common effort for Jewish culture; he had no interest in that. What was he interested in? Writing. Writing and being translated into English."

Shneiderman's wife knew Bashevis in Warsaw. She was still a child, but she wasn't particularly fond of him. He was in his own world, as it were; he didn't mix much with people, he was closed off, it was hard to get to know him. She could feel that as a child.

"He treated women very differently from men. He gravitated more toward women. I knew his wife well, the one he had a child with, Runia. She is still living. In Haifa. I met her in 1946, in the summer, after the Kielce pogrom, when she and her son had come back to Warsaw from the Soviet Union. I had gone to see the people who were returning from Russia. And I met her at the train station.

"Her name was Poncz, Runia Poncz. Was she pretty? Ugly, very ugly, but interesting. A smart, intelligent Communist. He didn't like Communists at all, yet he was with her. They were never officially a married couple, but they lived together. Her brother died in Spain during the civil war. I helped her out in Warsaw in 1946. I went to the Joint, the Jewish aid organization, and helped them settle down. She spoke Polish very well. 'Tell Itzhok that I'm here,' she told me.

"I came to New York, I phoned him. 'I met Runia, I saw your son,' I said, 'I've helped them; now you have to do something.' And this is what he answered me: 'Shneiderman, thank you for what you've done, but I beg you, in future don't inject yourself into my personal affairs.'

"In 1976 I was the president of the Jewish section of the PEN Club in New York, and I got a letter, as I did every year, asking me to nominate candidates for the Nobel Prize. I had several candidates: first Grade, second Sutzkever, third Bashevis. I wrote a letter to the executive committee, suggesting that this year the Nobel Prize should be awarded to Yiddish literature in general. As a symbolic award in recognition of the entire literature of a people who had suffered greatly during the war. A literature that is not pacifist, I won't say that, but that completely ignores armies. Created by a people who for so many years have been deprived of their own fatherland. And I sent off my proposal. I received a letter in reply saying that it was a very interesting idea, that the possibility had been discussed, but that it's against the rules, so please describe specific candidates. I supplied them with biographical sketches and bibliographies for each writer. I phoned Bashevis to tell him about this and to ask him for a bibliography of his writings. '*Bist meshuga?*' he said. 'Are you crazy? A Nobel Prize for me?' But I know he was just pretending to be astonished because he had been working toward that end for several years. Not himself; through his publisher Straus. 'I don't have a bibliography, don't start me dreaming, don't start yourself dreaming. You're wasting your time.' And two years later he won the Nobel.

"I remember that in 1977 in Israel I visited Sutzkever, and he said to me, 'Shneiderman, I have news for you. Your close friend is a serious candidate for the Nobel Prize.' I replied, 'I know, Bashevis!' Sutzkever was certain I was thinking it was *him*.

"Did people tell Bashevis their stories? No, that's a literary device. Would I have told him the story of my life? Never! We met quite often, but he never asked me how my life was going, nor did I ask him. We weren't friends. We would talk about writers, gossip a bit; he would complain about the *Forward,* about its editors, and make fun of Sutzkever.

"What is his wife like? Nondescript. First of all, she doesn't understand Yiddish; she's a German Jew. She's not interested in literature. She sold dresses in a department store, a housewife. He always said that he flirted with other women. Did he really flirt? Yes, she didn't stop him. She always left when young women came to interview him.

"We saw Bashevis two years ago in Florida when he was already very ill. He had Alzheimer's. He was finished. He looked at us, grabbed my arm; he obviously recognized me for a moment, but only for a moment. . . .

"At his funeral they all talked about themselves, only about themselves. And everyone spoke in English. Rabbi Berkowitz. His son. No one spoke Yiddish."

The Shneidermans lived in the same building in Nowolipki. She was the girl in the window; he lived across from her. But they actually met in journalism school. They have been together for over half a century.

"We are the last of the Mohicans."

They are weary; both of them are weary.

SHE: "I am tormented by memories. Too many years, too many years."

HE: "I no longer have the courage to live. I am the last one. They've all died; I buried them. It is so hard to be the last."

SHE: "I would like my husband to publish a collection of his letters, articles, sketches, poems. He doesn't want to. He says there's no one to publish for. Not a single new reader has emerged."

The rescuing of ashes—Samuel Shneiderman does not think it makes any sense.

MIAMI, 1992   Professor Heszel Klepfisz is a historian. In the preface to his book someone wrote, "Had I lived in prewar Poland, he would have been my rabbi."

"I can still name the dates of the reigns of every Polish king from Mieszko the First to Stanisław August Poniatowski. I have a great deal of respect for Polish history. During the years 1934 to '36 I published a Polish-language weekly, *Jewish Echoes*, in Warsaw. It was a religious paper. I remember that I also wrote an essay, 'Jewish Characters in Polish Literature.'

"I attended the Tachkemoni Rabbinical Seminary in Warsaw. That gave me the right to study at the university. I wrote in Polish and Yiddish. Polish Jews lived *with* Poles, not just among Poles. *With* them. Not everyone, of course, but many. Not only assimilated Jews, like the poets Julian Tuwim or Antoni Słonimski, but people like me, conscious, religious Jewish nationalists. My father spoke Russian; after all, he lived under the Russian occupation. But we had many Polish books in our house. We bought Polish newspapers. We lived *with* Poland, not just in Poland.

"I lived on Miła Street, on Bonifraterska. Warsaw was

my place on earth. Miła was a typical Jewish street. The only Poles who lived there were janitors. There is a wonderful novella by Maria Konopnicka, *Mendel Gdański*. It describes a pogrom in Warsaw in the 1880s. Mendel is attacked by Warsaw students and says at one point, 'My heart has died for the city of Warsaw.' How this was possible he cannot understand: 'They attacked me as if I were a foreigner! Warsaw was a part of my life.' That in fact is how many Polish Jews felt.

"The pogrom that took place in Kielce in 1946 is the Poles' greatest ignominy. To kill Jews after the war, after such a tragedy. That convinced me that my decision not to return to Poland was correct. I think this is one of the most shameful events in Polish history. I have read a lot about this; I never heard anything about its being a Russian provocation or that the Soviets were involved. In the Katyń massacre, yes, but not in Kielce. If that could be proved, it would remove a bitter odium from Polish history, from the Polish conscience.

"I remember the *Literary News*. I remember the Polish Jewish writers—Tuwim, Słonimski. I am a part of Poland. I served in the army with the essayist Ksawery Pruszyński. I have many documents recognizing me for my service in the Polish Army, decorations for my Polish patriotism. I was not alone. There were many were like me.

"No, I never wrote about Singer. That's filth.

"Is he a good guide to the world of Polish Jewry? No, a bad one. The worst possible. He knows how to tell a marvelous story, that's all. But the world he presents has very little in common with reality. Or with religion either.

"What Singer describes is folklore. Demons, dybbuks, devils: These are the beliefs of primitive people; they're fictions. Singer fantasizes. He doesn't write the truth; he invents. My father didn't commit all those filthy acts that religious Jews, even rabbis, do in Singer. Even his rabbis have a dark side to them. Except perhaps for his own father. They are base, aggressive, sinful. What he describes is a world of sin and crime; it is beyond my imagination. And it strays from the truth. My family were people, living people, with flaws, with shortcomings, but decent, worthy of respect. Living in harmony with tradition, devoted to religion, good Polish patriots, and not the types you find in Singer: degenerates, abnormal, sick people.

"The majority of Jewish shops were closed on Saturday; they were locked up already on Friday evening. Sometimes you had to wait until Monday because on Sunday, the Catholic holy day, Jews were forbidden to engage in trade. Ninety percent of Polish Jews observed the Sabbath laws. And that was a peculiar devotion, because after all, they were very poor, but they devoted themselves to religion. Jewish law forbade them to trade on Saturdays. It was unthinkable to open a shop on the Sabbath. That is strength of character. Why doesn't Singer write about that? Why doesn't he see it? They could barely keep body and soul together. Bread was a dream in many Jewish families, including my own. But an idea was more important than material profit.

"The famous Spanish philosopher Ortega y Gasset said: 'I exist in concrete circumstances, in a specific context.' There is no absolute 'I.' A writer must know why he is writing and for whom; that is Singer's great sin, that he did not answer that question for himself. Every descendant of Polish Jews must feel the same as I do about his writing.

"All my books are dedicated to the memory of my deceased parents, my brothers, my sisters. His mother and brother also perished. That is even worse evidence against him.

"Fifty years have passed. Everything has changed. My Polish is rusty now. I haven't spoken Polish for years. But on my bookshelf in Jerusalem you'll find the Romantic poetry of Juliusz Słowacki in a three-volume postwar Polish edition."

"Who is a Jew?"

"And who is a Pole? According to religious dictates, you have to be the son of a Jewish mother and profess Judaism. But there are people who think of themselves as Jews even if their mothers were not Jewish. Joseph Conrad lived outside Poland; he wrote in English, but he thought of himself as a Pole. Tuwim was a Pole, but during the war he wrote his essay 'We, the Polish Jews.' I think a Jew is simply someone who feels deep in his soul that he is a Jew. Yes, even without religion. Is a Polish Catholic only someone who practices Catholicism? I'm not sure. I think that the most important thing is the sense of belonging to a people even if one is not religious.

"Religious people believe that there is another world and punishment for sins. The distinction between Christianity and Judaism rests on the fact that Christians describe both heaven and hell, and the Jewish religion says that this is a mystery. But the idea is the same. Christianity is the daughter of Judaism.

"Were it not for the Kielce pogrom, there would still be about one hundred thousand Jews in Poland. In 1968 those who'd stayed on after Kielce were expelled. I ask you why. No other nation did this to their Jews after the war. Not one. That closed the door. It closed the chapter."

THERE WAS TOO MUCH MEMORY

ISRAEL, 1991   The heroes of my journey to the Holy Land could be his heroes or the cousins or kinfolk of his protagonists. They lived through that part of Jewish fate that he was spared.

Over there in Poland people always told them, "You are foreign," but they felt at home. Here they say, "You are at home," but they often feel foreign. In any random gathering of people in Haifa, Tel Aviv, Jerusalem, there is always someone from Lublin, Białystok, or Warsaw. The Przysucha rabbi's grandson or a relative of an innkeeper from Lubartów. The son of a friend of the Communist leader Nowotko or the daughter of the tailor from the Biłgoraj market. In every group there is someone from Pawia or Dzika, from Krochmalna or Marszałkowska streets. At the seaside, at a party, in an almost empty railway car in the outskirts of Nazareth, in the vicinity of Tsvat or Beersheva, where all languages are spoken, one can always count on hearing a more or less rusty Polish.

In Israel, there are several hundred thousand Jews of Polish origin.

They left because "there was too much memory."

They left because they "didn't want to be guilty of everything."

They left because they were expelled.

They left with bitterness.

Here they often dream of landscapes with weeping willows and of pierogi with blueberries. They remember the aroma of Polish words, because only they, no others, have an aroma. Poland remains an aching wound.

Mordechai Canin thinks that the only place where Jews live in Poland is the Jewish cemetery on Gęsia Street in Warsaw.

He comes from the little town of Sokołów Podlaski, an hour and a half ride from Warsaw. He has read all the Polish classics in Yiddish translation. The grandson of a pious Jew, he wept while reading the patriotic novels of Henryk Sienkiewicz. From age fourteen he was educated in Warsaw, on Dzielna Street, but the building doesn't exist anymore. He studied with Rabbi Sokołowski, a great rabbi.

Canin's landscape was a Polish landscape. There he could smell the earth; here he cannot smell it.

"The loss of Poland is a greater loss for me than the loss of my mother. Because if I lose my mother, I know that I will follow her there. This loss is irreversible.

"The Jewish people became a real people through Jewish literature. A people without a land. But it turns out that one can live without a land. My land is my soul. What I merged with in my youth, the richness of the literature, that is mine. And the rest? It makes no difference where I live. Memory?

Yes, but I am incapable of separating it from the graves. I regret that I didn't end up in the ovens too, because I bear the punishment inside me—that tragedy. Here they accepted reparations from the Germans, but is there reparation for something like that?"

Mordechai Canin writes about his people, what they were like. He is torn.

"I live in Israel, and I am an Israeli citizen, but this is not my motherland. I lost my motherland. Not Poland in its entirety, with its Polish anti-Semitism, but Polish Jewry. Unfortunately the Poles never wanted to know the Jews. They saw only haggling shopkeepers. They didn't see the Jewish soul, even though there were great Polish poets of Jewish origin."

Yael feels that as a people they are always wandering in the desert. She has been here since 1948. Officially she is definitely in her own country. Emotionally too it seems that she is at home. But she believes that everyone here has a schizophrenic attitude toward Poland. For her, Hebrew words don't have color or brilliance, even though it is the language she uses every day, the only language in which she converses with her son. Nonetheless, when he calls her Ima, she doesn't feel like a mama.

Nachman has lived in Israel for thirty-five years. For twenty-five years he felt like a newcomer, because he yearned for the old.

"For me, Poland is a beloved country, the country I remember from my childhood. Today Poland is for me one large

Jewish cemetery. I go back to Auschwitz from time to time to leave stones in memory of the dead. Remember this—I am trying not to forget the words of the dying."

He comes from Dęblin, his wife from Ryki. They gather at the cemetery every year with other people from that town. On the day of annihilation. For a communal Kaddish.

Before the war, in Poland, he was a third-class citizen, not even second-class. Third. He wasn't assigned to officers' training school only because he was a Jew. Today he wonders why he didn't protest. They were a minority. Here it's the same thing; they don't induct Arabs into the armed forces.

He has no good memories from Poland even though a Pole rescued him in the forest. He still would like to find the man. After liberation men from the underground Home Army killed two of his friends.

This is his country, his place. His corner of the world. Only they are being driven out of here too. In Poland people said, "Jews to Palestine!" And here: "Get out!"

He remembers taking a room for the night after the war not far from his hometown. The proprietress offered him tea. All of a sudden she said, "I can't bring myself to kill a fly on the wall, but I would have killed Jews without batting an eye." That he remembers, although he knows there are other Poles too, they have trees in Yad Vashem.

"I remember my grandfather, but he was atypical because he was a farmer. I remember the goat that overturned the seder table; my brother and I had let her into the house as the prophet Elijah. That was in Ukraine. Mama spoke Yiddish with us children, but she also spoke Polish and Russian. Father was a Communist; Mother was very pious. On Saturday Father would escort Mama to the synagogue, and on Yom Kippur he would take us to Kraków for cake. Father spent time in prisons. Mama fasted, begged God to have mercy, but nothing came of it.

They both died during the war: Father was killed in the street, and Mother in the ghetto."

"My attitude toward Poland is very complicated," says Łucja. "I always defend Poland. Before the war there were no anti-Semitic excesses in my school. This was in Warsaw; the school was founded by Maria Skłodowska-Curie. There, if one of the girls was an anti-Semite, she would have had to hide it. In the village where we lived, I didn't feel any anti-Semitism either.

"But I remember that when I wanted to hear Professor Wacław Borowy lecture on Polish literature at Warsaw University, a crowd of students were standing in front of the doors, letting some people in, but not others. 'Go in, colleague, go on in,' I heard. 'We're not letting Jews in.' 'I'm going in,' I said, 'because this is my university.' 'Don't cry, miss,' a policeman said. 'This will pass. It's a phase.' That was in 1936.

"I never concealed the fact that I was Jewish, but I was often taken for a Christian. For instance, in a train before the war someone said, '*You* won't have any difficulty getting accepted into the university.'

"I had what was called a good face. I remember an incident from the very beginning of the war, right after the Germans invaded Warsaw. I'm walking along Polna Street, a group of Germans are ahead of me, and some fat Pole walks past me. Suddenly he turns and yells in the direction of the Germans, 'You lousy Jewess!' The Germans didn't react. If that had happened two years later, they would have killed me.

"I think that a Pole's cultural level can be measured by his attitude toward Jews. I never say 'Polack,' and I don't let anyone say 'Kike.' I think that we love Poland with an unrequited love. Because we consider ourselves part Polish, but the Poles don't want us.

"I remember the following scene in Russia, in Tajikistan in 1941. We were registering Polish nationals in the region. A man walks in who couldn't possibly be taken for anything but a Jew. He's short, hunchbacked, a worker; his surname is Zygier. And he stands there and recites Mickiewicz's defiant patriotic poem 'Ordon's Redoubt.' The teacher on the podium cries. Another time a patriarchal Jew came in, handsome, old, bearded, and he spoke of Poland with such emotion that I asked him, 'How come, why? It's different for me: I'm from a Polonized background; I was raised on Polish literature, in the Polish language. But you? Why should you love Poland so dearly? Please explain this to me.' And then he said something that I will never forget as long as I live: 'Our Polish brothers were evil, but Poland our mother was good.' "

His maternal grandfather was a renowned Talmudist. His mother was progressive, and she knew how to write in Polish. As a boy he attended Gymnasium on Saturdays too, so the Hasidim threw his father out of the synagogue.

He remembers the great pogrom in Lwów in 1918 and the arrival of General Haller's army. He remembers Jabotinsky, the Zionist leader, and how he came to Poland and shouted, "Get out, Jews, get out of Poland because extermination awaits you here." They didn't listen. They didn't want to leave their five-room apartments and Polish servants. He remembers the reforms enacted by Minister of the Treasury Władysław Grabski in 1925 and is truly grateful to him. Because even though he destroyed Jewish business in Poland with his taxes, he developed Tel Aviv. It was built by Polish Jews. Tel Aviv is the work of Minister Grabski.

And he remembers another incident. In the Tarnobrzeg Gymnasium, where he was a teacher, "I was introducing an excerpt from Professor Ignacy Chrzanowski's history of Polish literature. About Mikołaj Rej. That Rej was the first to write in Polish, because up until that time Polish was the language of the rabble. At that moment—I remember it as if it were today—my best student, Jan Prędzki, stood up and said, 'Jews are the rabble.' Had someone else been in my place, perhaps he might have taken it, but I answered him immediately: 'You boor. You and your people didn't even exist when that "rabble" gave you your God in whom you believe. Get out of here.'

"Sometime after that a notice appeared in the local newspaper: 'Look what we've come to, we Poles, that a Jew, a Moses, should be teaching our Catholic children Polish.' "

It was the first and last time that happened to him. Four years before the war began he left Poland. He is a professor at the university in Jerusalem.

" 'How much bread have you baked?' 'How many trees have you planted?' We used to ask each other such questions in the beginning in Israel. In my first kibbutz I was a baker."

Leon Harari also planted trees. Like everyone. He planted them by day, and at night the Bedouins would tear out the seedlings or trample them. They didn't want to have a green fatherland.

"In Poland, despite the fact that I worked on the *Little Review,* which was a periodical for Jewish youth, and that my friends were Jews, of course what I thought about was integration. Not just assimilation but integration. I joined the Polish Socialist party in order not to be in a Jewish organization, but as it turned out, the Poles didn't want integration. I was one of the secretaries in the Old Town district of Warsaw; I was seventeen at the time. 'What!' people would say. 'That Jew represents the PSP?' "

Today he has no illusions, and he wouldn't even think of remaining among the goyim, of living with them. He believes that nowadays a Jew who lives in Germany, in Poland, or anywhere but Israel is a renegade. He thinks this way after what happened during the war. He cannot understand how anyone could remain there.

"For me, Poland is a cemetery."

"Just a cemetery?"

"Just a cemetery.

"Nostalgia? For what? My first language is Hebrew; my second is probably German. What has remained of Polish culture has penetrated me deeply, but I don't know if I will pass it on to anyone. To whom?

"Poland wronged me. These are things that cannot heal. A thin film may grow over them, but then some Miss Tuszyńska shows up and rips it off. In every one of us there is a certain amount of masochism. Whether we want to or not, we like it to be ripped open, probed.

"Sentiment? Nalewki, Gęsia, Smocza, Pawia, Zamenhof: Those streets, those courtyards with communal wells where thousands of families lived in one apartment. In one bed, four children, three, their little arms and legs intertwined. What should I feel nostalgic about? That poverty?

"I lived in the Old Town, not in the best conditions, in a building on the corner of Kamienne Schodki Street. There were fifty-odd tenants, and we had two terribly filthy toilets. The lines formed early in the morning, and the entire gallery of all the tenants stood there in front of those toilets. Only the landlady, Gębarzewska, had her own toilet. The public one was always covered with shit, filthy; there were rats in the courtyard. What should I be nostalgic about? That's pure claptrap. Sometimes I'm nostalgic for Tuwim, for Słonimski, the lectures in the Union of Freethinkers at Eighteen Karowa Street. Or for young Jan Twardowski, with whom I used to stroll for hours on end through the Old Town while he recited his poems to me. That's my Warsaw. Forlorn.

"Once—it was in 1932 or 1933—I was beaten up in the Old Town. Some punks attacked me on Wąski Dunaj Street. I went up to a policeman, and he laughed. I told the writer Igor Newerly about this; he was editor of the *Little Review*. Newerly phoned Janusz Korczak: 'What should we do, Doctor?'

"And Korczak answered, 'Write about it on the front page of the *Little Review*.'

"So I wrote that I, a Polish patriot, with a father who was in the trenches in 1914, a brother in the army, that I, a loyal citizen, was beaten up. The next week someone wrote a response to my article. And that response was confiscated. What was in it? In brief: that those who beat up little Jews during the week go to church on Sunday and pray to a big Jew.

"How is a Jew different from a Pole? A Jew is more cynical. He has had so much unpleasant experience; he has endured so much; there have been so many Golgothas among the Jews. Jewish suffering has been inflicted for two thousand years of history. Pacifications, pogroms, murders, the Holocaust, ghettos. The Jews who live in Poland today, even in America, even in France, will never rid themselves of their Jewish complex. A complex doesn't just develop in the course of a single day. It is like baker's yeast; it rises. We can't rid ourselves of it. That is why I say that a Jew today, with no illusions after what happened in the thirties and up to 1945, can live only in Israel and nowhere else."

He came here in 1939. He actually swam the last meters. He is one of the founders of Kibbutz Maale HaHamisha, which was built on the spot where five people were killed while planting trees in the desert.

In the train to Haifa I sit next to an elderly gentleman who is reading a French book. After a while it turns out that his father was from Międzyrzecze and his mother from Biała Podlaska. We continue conversing in French because they left Poland in 1922, and he remembers only two words. He remembers them from a visit to Warsaw in 1939, on vacation. He was walking down Gęsia and Nalewki streets, eating ice cream (*Lody, lody za pięć groszy*—"Ice cream, ice cream for five groschen") and sizing up the young ladies with his friend. *Ładna dziewczynka!* "A pretty girl!" A lot of people have preserved that one expression in their memory. A lot of people addressed me as *ładna dziewczynka*, and it had nothing to do with my age. It froze them in a time that signified their youth or Poland, or sometimes both the one and the other.

In Beit Lohamei Hagetaot I ate poppy seed cake, hot and fresh from the large kibbutz oven. A poppy seed cake baked by Meir Krasnostawski from Korec in Volhynia, whose father was a baker and a confectioner. The best poppy seed cake I have ever eaten.

Małka, a pious Jewish woman from Kiryat Ata—the one whose father, Isaac Meir Korman, did nothing but write, and when he died, they announced his death on the radio—allows me to sample her cinnamon raisin kugel. She hasn't spoken Polish for more than fifty years. She tells me in rusty Polish, "I know all the word, but they lack me." She wears a wig; she observes the Sabbath; she is happy that she is a Jew, but it is very difficult. When she was in Poland, people would mention Palestine to her, but "I was a Pole, I remember President Mościcki and Marshal Piłsudski; I remember how they died and we wept in school and wore black armbands on our sleeves." She remembers some Polish songs. And the courtyard on Lubartowska Street in Lublin. The synagogue at No. 30 and the Chapel of Mary and Jesus at No. 16.

I ate gefilte fish a number of times. I was also treated to Polish words.

"In Poland," says Tadeusz, "I always had to explain that I had not personally participated in the crucifixion of Christ. And here, that not all Poles are anti-Semites."

His wife's grandfather was a peddler. He sold haberdashery in villages throughout the Lublin region: suspenders, buttons, handkerchiefs, thread. He spent his entire life on the road, trading with Poles. And he never had anything bad to say about them. If a Jew were to enter an Arab village here, he would be beaten up in a minute.

He lived on the corner of Gęsia and Zamenhof streets. His father owned a hosiery store. He was born and raised in the Jewish ghetto, and all his energy was focused on getting out of there. To escape, at any price. He remembers the struggle at home, the terrible struggle to stay afloat and to maintain appearances—for example, that they have fish on the Sabbath. Jews were not admitted to the public Gymnasium; private schools were expensive. His studies were paid for with his mother's sealskin coat. When he brought home Bs from school, his father would tell him, "You can't afford this luxury; you have to be better because you are starting out worse." Learning, education—that was opportunity. But there was a price. Yes, he'll become a doctor, but he'll stop being one of us, he'll start reading disgraceful books. On the first Yom Kippur after his graduation his father begged him, "Drop by the synagogue," so the neighbors wouldn't think his son was a complete heretic. Immediately afterward he and his friends went straight from Nalewki Street to the Old Town to feast on pork.

He couldn't attend the public Gymnasium. He wasn't drafted into the army. He didn't take part in the September campaign. He couldn't participate in Polish life as he wanted to. He couldn't experience Polish history. This is where his two fates went their separate ways: Jewish and Polish.

I walk into a supermarket on Weizman Street in Tel Aviv. I pick up some soap and juice, that's all, and stand in line. The elderly man who is ahead of me starts saying something in Hebrew. I don't understand. He gestures; he wants to let me go first. I thank him in all the languages I know; finally, using my one remaining life raft, in Polish. It never fails. He is from Radom; he left in 1935. No, he hasn't been back since then, and he has no desire to go there. At one point a woman with a shopping cart, who is standing next to us, says something in Hebrew in a loud voice. This goes on for quite some time. I can sense the unpleasant tone, and I want to retreat to the end of the line. "What is she saying?" I ask in Polish. "I'll tell you what she is saying," she answers in Polish. "She says that during the war the Poles were worse than the Germans; she says that they went around handing over Jews, that they derived a diabolical pleasure from pointing them out. For a bottle of vodka or for free." She goes on saying that she refuses to use that language, that she won't read books, that she doesn't want to hear anything about them.

I walk out. Across the street is the local lottery office. The man inside is a Jew from Romania. We chat for a while in French, and when he finds out that I'm from Poland, he says, naturally, *"Ładna dziewczynka."* "Give God a chance, buy a lottery ticket." I don't buy one because Irena, who hasn't spoken Polish in ever so many years and absolutely must talk with me right now, approaches me. A moment later we are drinking coffee at a little round table. Under a palm tree. In the center of the city. And she tells me her story. That day Polish words elicit other Polish words. Without any help from me.

"I used to ask myself how I would have acted, whether I would have rescued Poles if my family and I were threatened with the death penalty. I don't know what I would have done. Someone who has not lived through it can be critical, filled with hatred. I knew a Polish woman, Józefa K., who rescued Jews. Because of this, her husband was killed by the Home Army. There are all sorts of fish in a river. I survived the war in Russia. I lost my father in Majdanek, in the death camp, my sister in the Białystok ghetto. We returned to Poland, to Lower Silesia, from Magnitogorsk in 1946; we got established there. We believed there would be a Poland. I worked in a city-owned department store in Wrocław. It was hard; there were very few goods, sometimes none at all. People said, 'The Jewesses are stealing, and the Jewish men are drinking our blood! Jews to Palestine!' And when the children came home from nursery school and asked what 'lousy Jew' means, I knew that I could not stay there. My husband and I left with our four children. In 1956.

"I don't know if the Poles helped Hitler. I feel ashamed for those who gave people up and didn't have to do that. I am not angry that they didn't hide people; after all, it could have cost them their lives. But to hand people over for a kilo of sugar or a loaf of bread . . ."

At an adjacent table there is a woman in a red blouse and white and black beads; I have the feeling that she has been listening in on our conversation for some time.

"But the Poles delighted in doing this," she insists; "they were worse than the Germans."

"How can you say that! Please, don't get upset." Irena protects me.

"They handed people over when their money ran out. They accepted it until the very end and then handed them over to their death. They called Jews 'cats.'"

An elderly, balding man in a light-colored jacket and blue shirt is seated at the same table.

"I smuggled moonshine on the Warsaw-Otwock line," he interjects. "I was a vodka supplier. I had so much money in my pockets that I could have eaten in the best restaurant, but I ate under the Kierbedź Bridge for twenty groschen. Do you know why? I was afraid of the Poles."

The woman in the red blouse survived the Radom ghetto; the man, her husband, survived Majdanek. They live in Paris. He owns a wholesale outlet on rue St. Denis.

HE: "I don't want to go to Poland. It means nothing to me. Nothing."

At one point he takes his wallet and pulls out a scrap of paper that is tucked in among his credit cards: "Number thirty-four Tatary Łąki. There was a side street by that name; that's where my property was located."

SHE: "Don't go back to Poland, miss. By no means. Nothing good awaits you there." That day I don't speak any more Polish.

"We were torn from the soil," says Itka, "and packed into flower pots. Usually they weren't ugly. That softened the shock. But we were accustomed to the soil. Israeli identity is a way of destroying the past. After all, it is an artificial fatherland. And that's the injustice of it.

"We can't be tourists in Poland. That's why we don't go.

"Franciszkańska Street, Ciasna Street, Miła Street—we used to write those words in our Hebrew classes, using the biblical alphabet. We fell in love with Jerusalem, Nazareth, Ramat Gan. But here in Israel there are no willow trees."

As a student at Warsaw University, Professor S. for an entire year remained standing on the odd side of the hall during lectures. His colleagues from the Polish Socialist party stood with him, and the students from the ONR Camp, who were radical nationalists, would wait after class for the students from the odd side and their supporters to come out. His student passbook was stamped "Jew." That was during the 1938–39 academic year. He remembers that the only professor who stood with them was the philosophy professor Tadeusz Kotarbiński. Were it not for Professor Kotarbiński, he doubts that he could have spoken with Poles at all. The humiliation was too intense. Kotarbiński gave him back his faith in man.

"At home I was the only son; whatever I wanted, I got. I remember that I wanted a squirrel. But we had red squirrels, and I wanted a black squirrel. There weren't any black squirrels in our district near Zamość. So my father traveled to Krakow and then to Vienna and brought me back a black squirrel in a cage. We had woods, and beyond the woods there was a pond. And that squirrel escaped into the woods. I cried. They bought me a pony. To console me."

In the fall of 1942 a boy in short trousers, the same boy who had dreamed of a squirrel and whose dream was fulfilled, found himself all alone in the woods. For two months he wandered around the Rakszawa region where his parents had owned a sawmill and a flour mill before the war. He slept in a mortuary, but one evening he found a corpse on the catafalque and decided to turn himself in to the police. A neighbor from Potok, a Mr. Panek, restrained him and promised to hide him.

Rafał Goldberg spent twenty-two months in the attic of a woolens mill. When he came out, he was unable to walk. There were two other Jewish families there: the Silbersteins and the Ferbers. Five people knew about their hiding place.

Józef Frączek was one of them. He was posthumously awarded the medal of the Righteous among the Nations. He didn't take a single grosch from the Jews. He fed them and protected them. He endangered the lives of his wife and four sons. On Catholic holidays, Rafał remembers, all the children received holiday packets of candies.

Goldberg doesn't know if there is a limit to what a man can endure. He refers to his own situation as "a spa." But it taught him good humor. He can laugh. He is incapable of worrying. He knows that he could lose everything in an instant. And that one has to keep on living.

The first word that Menachem S. heard in his life was a Polish word. Polish was the language of the intelligentsia, of assimilated Jews. The lullaby that his mother sang to him was a

Polish lullaby. That was on Elektoralna Street near Bankowy Square in Warsaw. That's where he was born. His father owned a store there; he was a jeweler. That's where Menachem went to school—on the corner of Walicόw Street.

"We don't consider ourselves part of the Polish Diaspora here, nor do we consider ourselves émigrés. What is the difference between us and the emigration in the rest of the world? We *go back.* The Polish newspaper that is published here isn't a Polish newspaper in Israel; it's an Israeli newspaper in the Polish language. Its readership is dying out, and there will never be any new ones. There are no more Polish Jews. Those several thousand old folks in Poland aren't going to come here.

"There are no Jews in Poland, but the Jew has become the incarnation of an abstract evil. Like the devil, shall we say. Anti-Semitism might have had some foundation before the war, when there were three and a half million Jews in a population of thirty-five million, but now the enemy does not exist. Instead Poland, an object of hatred, whether real or imagined, exists in reality.

"The attitude toward Poland among those of us who came from there is hostile, but it shouldn't be confused with our attitude toward the language. That would be like refusing to speak German because Hitler spoke German. German is also the language of Goethe and Schiller. The attitude toward Poland here is unfriendly, even antagonistic.

"People say that Poles suck anti-Semitism with their mother's milk. That is blatant nonsense. Only vitamins, fat, and water can be sucked in with mother's milk. Everything else comes from one's upbringing."

"In Poland a Jew couldn't be a policeman, or a streetcar motorman, or even a building superintendent. So he had to be a doctor or a lawyer."

The Jewish poet David Opatoshu recalled the aroma of Polish forests. The Vistula whispered to Sholem Asch in Yiddish. Both are no longer alive.

"How many countries are there in the world," someone reflects, "where there is an Umschlagplatz and also the hill of the doomed in Płaszów, a Gęsia Street, Treblinka and Kock, Przysucha, Góra Kalwaria, Oświęcim-Auschwitz?"

In Israel there are roughly a hundred writers who write in Polish. They have their own union, and they publish two literary journals. In Israel on Allenby Street there is the Edmund Neustein Bookstore, the best-stocked Polish bookstore I have ever seen, including a used-book store and a literary salon. But Poland has no heirs here. The people have no one to leave their large libraries to, with their volumes of Mickiewicz, Żeromski, Tuwim. The grandchildren barely understand Polish.

In the Holy Land both languages of the Diaspora Jews—Yiddish and Polish—met the same fate.

Stanisław Wygodzki came to Israel in 1968 and knew, the moment he landed here, that he was finished as a poet. He hasn't written a single line in Hebrew; he hasn't even tried. Twenty-three years later he repeats, "Actually I still haven't left Poland." In a little bag he keeps a handful of earth from the hillside below the Warsaw Citadel. Polish books and Polish memories. That's how he survives. One of the last. His family spoke Polish, Yiddish, and Hebrew at home. They ate challah and fish and chicken broth with noodles, but they also ate ham and smoked pork sausage. He thinks that the most delicious ham is eaten on Yom Kippur. He doesn't care about the stones around here. Or about Jerusalem. He is from Puszcza Białowieska, Poland's primeval forest.

"A Communist system, so-called real communism, was the dream of my youth, because I was a Jew. The Jews were a significant minority in Silesia before the war, yet the stigma of belonging to the Jewish people was quite apparent, even if it wasn't painful. A yearning to eliminate this inequality led me to communism. Because communism was supposed to disentangle all these questions of anti-Semitism and inequality.

"I am a Polish writer living in Israel. I am ashamed of Poland and of Polish anti-Semitism. I am a Jew who is ashamed. But I cannot hate Poland. I can hate a particular individual who sold a person in hiding for half a liter of vodka."

Wanda is a former courier for Żegota, the wartime underground organization that distributed aid to Jews in hiding. Today she works as a teacher. In a Hebrew school. All her friends went to the ovens. She used to attend meetings of Jews from Poland in the hope that she would find someone, but that hardly ever happens anymore. It didn't happen to her. She is head of the Union of Varsovians, who are dying out, whose numbers are steadily diminishing. They are trying to publish a book about Jewish Warsaw, but they never have enough money. The union, dependent on its members' contributions, cannot expand its activities. Their largest gathering is on April 19, the anniversary of the Warsaw Ghetto Uprising. It is very warm. They remember the weather in Warsaw. Then.

Wanda travels to Poland with young people who were born in Israel. She goes there to show them the little towns, the cemeteries, the death camps. She thinks this is necessary, even essential. Because in order to see the sun, they first have to see the ovens. It may be a torment to live with such baggage, but she thinks it is indispensable.

The kibbutzim youth whom she knows are interested in this. Those trips derive from their inner needs. It was a very complicated process. The young people felt pity for their parents, who came here and fell silent. The parents had difficulties with work, with the language, with apartments. They wanted, somehow, to enter into this society, which lives an entirely different life and is occupied with entirely different problems. Wanda was never able to explain to those young people how it was possible that such a perfect death machine could have existed. Their parents had the same problem explaining it, so they withdrew, fell silent, unable to scream. But the young people woke up by themselves. Today they want to know.

They work for a year in the fields, harvesting fruit, making sauerkraut, planting flowers, and that's how they earn enough money to pay for their trip to Poland. They are sixteen years old, not yet of draft age; most of them have one more year of high school ahead of them. This is a revolution in their lives. They come back transformed. She doesn't know for how long.

There were no legends in their families, no treasured memories. No one drew family trees. But before their departure a few of them were told by their mothers about a wooden porch in a house in Lubartów or a grandfather's tombstone not far from the village of Parchatka. A courtyard with an alcove in which they used to hide as children. A street sign. It evoked the strongest emotions, remembered addresses, places, houses, gardens. Because millions are an abstraction. Even piles of shoes and hair are impersonal. The students lit candles on thresholds, in meadows, in apartments in which they discovered furniture that they recognized from other people's descriptions.

These young people experience a hothouse childhood. From there they go directly into the regimentation of the army and the constant threat of war. They could die at any moment. Go and not return. These are communal children. If they are not Wanda's, then they are her neighbor's or her friend's. Through Poland they suddenly catch a glimpse of another world. They see war as meticulously prepared extermination. This cannot be experienced without an echo. Their mental horizons change. Certain values become dearer. Their attitude to the state changes: to one full of gratitude. They have their own country, their home, their place to which they can always return.

She remembers the reaction of one of the girls on a visit to the Majdanek concentration camp. "Wanda, this is terrifying," she said. "It's having no impact on me." She felt guilty. She condemned herself for her lack of tears. She broke down and cried on another occasion. "Why is that oven so small?" she had asked. "To economize on fuel; it was for the little children."

Wanda is afraid of gas, and that was the greatest shock for her during the recent war with Saddam. The possibility that it could happen again: It hangs over them like a sword.

Sometimes they still don't know who they are. There is a special column in the Polish newspaper: "Who knows who I am?"

"My adoptive parents were Anna and Maksymilian Kamiński, who lived in Skarżysko Kamienna. My present address is: Łucja Sęktas, Piaseczno near Warsaw."

Who knows who I am?

"My adoptive parents: Tokarz; they lived in Bochnia. My name: Janina Drozd. Please send any information to Mrs. Celina Łapowska, Haifa, Lotos 8."

Who knows who I am?

"As a child I was handed over by my parents to a Catholic family who lived near the railroad station in Jackowice near Łowicz, without a name, without a birth certificate. My father's name was Adam. If anyone knows anything about this, please write. Władysława Icewicz, 12 Antonówka Street, Kamienna Góra, Jelenia Góra province."

Sometimes they find out.

Her search lasted forty-five years. Israel and Esther gave their several-months-old little girl to the Stopnica church. They perished, burned to death in Auschwitz. Raised by Poles as Stanisława, at age forty-five she was discovered by relatives from Israel.

"I have lived on this earth for so many years, and only now do I learn the whole truth. I am terribly lost; I have to rediscover myself. I can't sleep or eat; I feel sick. Chaja Topiół."

In Yiddish songs everything happened on rooftops. Love on the roof, and happiness too. All staircases were on the outside, and they all led upward.

If you wanted to see your future, you went up to the roof. You went up to the roof when you fell in love. "You had to be superior, superior, in order to be equal. So, upward, to the rooftop, in order to emerge from below, in order to be someone."

In Israel today Yiddish songs are rarely sung.

A LETTER TO ME

Dear Pani Agata Tuszyńska:

I read your story "There Was Too Much Memory" with profound emotion. The same kind of emotion that accompanied my reading of Singer's books.

My entire family were nationalists. True, no one among my relatives ever persecuted anyone, but the atmosphere in which a young child grew up, the conversations of the grown-ups that fell upon "a child's great ear" made an impression.

After the war our sad reality also did not engender sympathy for our "older brothers." The secret police agents who came for my father were Jews. The military prosecutor who interrogated him for months on end was also a Jew. When I entered the army involuntarily after completing my studies, I met many Jewish colonels, but no noncommissioned officers, not to mention privates. Those were my experiences, but I did not welcome the anti-Semitic campaign of March 1968 with joy; quite the contrary—with sorrow and embarrassment.

Years later I contacted the Social-Cultural Society of Jews. I thought I would learn the language of our common Holy Scriptures. Unfortunately I learned only the alphabet and a bit of Yiddish. But I met with a great deal of kindness and goodwill. I wouldn't have written were it not for the fragment about Małka from Kiryat Ata in your book. She remembers "a courtyard on Lubartowska Street, the synagogue at No. 30, and the Chapel of Mary and Joseph at No. 16."

That is also my recollection. Deported from Gdynia and then from our apartment, which the Germans took a liking to, we moved into No. 18 Lubartowska Street in Lublin. Pani Małka does not name the city of her memories, but it was probably Lublin.

There, in the building that housed Lejb's bakery, I used to play with other children my age—all Jews. Later I saw the people driven into the ghetto, which began on the other side of Lubartowska Street. Then the dead were driven in large trucks to the Jewish cemetery in the Kalinowo district. Whole mountains of dead people. Protruding arms, legs. Once I saw a tiny child's foot wearing a white snow boot, just like the ones I had before the war. That image still haunts me though half a century has passed.

Dear Pani Agata, if you are in correspondence with the heroes of your reportage, please write to Pani Małka that there is someone in her first fatherland who was moved by her recollections, who feels close to her.

I was there several years ago. I walked the traces of the past.

Alas, the little chapel is no longer there. It was probably in someone's way.

W. R.

He was the first Jewish writer to describe man from head to toe, without skipping the middle. He said of himself, "Up to the waist, I am an angel, but from the waist down I am a devil."

He never tried to hide the fact that the Sixth Commandment was always the most difficult for him to obey.

In his works one step separates the synagogue from sex.

From the start he wrote about sex in a way that shocked the Jewish critics. He has an erotic scene in a carriage. There is an attempt at sex through a hole in the wall of a prison cell. There are thoughts about making love *à trois*. And a story about a countess who copulated with a stallion.

A Jewish girl goes to bed with her own father; another, with the man who murdered her family. A hunchback always has a parade of maidens coming to be with him, and a seventeen-year-old murderer of his own mother is raped in prison. Women teach their husbands all the little tricks they've learned from their lovers.

In *Satan in Goray* he writes that during the days of the false Messiah, Sabbatai Zevi, people indulged in all sorts of debauchery. At that time there lived in Pilice a teacher who had such a wild imagination that while he was praying, wrapped in his tallith, he was able to fantasize that he was copulating and actually have an ejaculation. The accursed sect considered this so great a talent that they chose him to be their leader.

He was ruthless toward his forebears. And, in his own way, shameless in endowing them with earthly desires. He was deceitful in offering temptations and indulgent toward those who succumbed to the whispers of Satan.

His rabbis have sinful thoughts, and his heroes not only break the commandments but also desecrate holy places and holy days.

Reb Amram (in "The Pocket Remembered") is visited in his dreams by a girl from the circus. Naked, with loose, fiery red hair. He indulges in erotic fantasies.

Aaron Greidinger (from *Shosha*) kisses Betty over a Torah scroll in a prayer house on Krochmalna Street. Asa Heshel, descendant of rabbis (*The Family Moskat*), spends Yom Kippur with another man's wife!

Singer blasphemed, provoked, desecrated everything holy. Not from a wish to shock but in the name of truth about the sorrows of human desires. He did this from the beginning. As early as *Satan in Goray* he describes a scene of the devil's perversions, to which Rachel submits: "He ravished her so many times that she was powerless to move." Some twenty years later he writes about Yasha, the hero of *The Magician of Lublin*: "Then afterwards he bore her into the alcove and drew the bedcurtains. He now made love to her so often and for such a long period of time that fear gripped her heart. He was clearly a warlock with the strength of the devil."

He described practically all categories, species, and variations of eroticism. And these are not the descriptions of a yeshiva boy. For the milieu from which he came, this was unacceptable. They would have repeated after Joseph Shapiro from *The Pen-*

itent that literature is nothing more than one great reference book of sexual perversions.

He dismissed as utter nonsense the belief that literature should ignore love and sex. Even the Bible and the Talmud are full of sex and love stories. There was nothing shameful about it; they were recognized as an inevitable part of life. Only in them, according to Singer, is the truth about man revealed. He wanted to penetrate it.

Singer's heroes are not ashamed of their bodies. They yield to their bodies' laws and transports. Religion calls the body a "vessel of shame and disgrace," a vessel of humiliation. That he took the measure of this conflict testifies to his bravery. And constitutes the modernity of that writing, even in those fragments that are covered by traditional Jewish clothing. "The rabbi is naked!" Singer seems to be saying, with a twinkle in his eye, like a nasty cheder boy. He didn't hesitate to say that "love of life is stronger than love of God. But faith in God is just as indispensable in life as sex."

He considered the passions the key to the world; man without emotions is only a chunk of wood. He marveled at God's generosity in endowing people with emotions and repeated after Spinoza that there is nothing in life that cannot become an obsession.

He was certain that every story is a love story.

He was certain that in virtually every matron a Madame Bovary lies sleeping.

He was certain that a man in the throes of passion is in the power of a dybbuk.

Singer knew that passion is suffering.

He explained that writing about a happy marriage, about a peaceful life as a couple, did not interest him. That it is not a fit subject for a book. He believed that literature should show obsessed characters, full of passion, because then one can see man in all his complexity of good and of evil. If everything is all right, Singer asked, what is there to write about? His protagonist is usually a bachelor, a divorced man, or a widower, almost always with the soul of a Don Juan.

"Women . . ." thought Max from *Scum,* "I shall try to have as many of them as possible. I won't spare money. I shall possess as many of them as I can."

Abram Shapiro from *The Family Moskat* grew old, put on weight, became sick. And yet . . . "His hand touched his groin. He was overtaken with desire. 'To have another woman,' he thought. 'Once more before I die.' He got back into bed and covered himself with the blanket. He chewed on another piece of the raisin bread."

They all spun similar dreams and fantasies. Asa Heshel from *The Family Moskat* saw himself "as a maharajah with eighteen wives, lovely women from India, Persia, Arabia, Egypt—and a few particularly beautiful Jewesses." "He began to think about the women he had had. If time is an illusion, as Kant believed, then he still had them. Somewhere, in a different sphere, he was living with Adele, with the daughter of the ritual slaughterer in Berne, the kindergarten teacher in Kiev, with Sonia on the estate near Ekaterinoslav." Sometimes he dreamed that he was lying with his sister Dinah and daughter Dacha. He even had an incestuous relationship with his mother. " 'What do they want of me?' he wondered. 'What kind of filth is there in my subconscious?' "

His men were sacrifices to their own philosophy, according to which the only thing that counted was pleasure. The delight of taking, not of giving.

They all were like that.

Yasha, who lived only for the moment, guided only by impulse and inspiration. Balancing between several women, experiencing the perverse pleasure of a pressured life and emotional chaos. Herman, his spiritual brother, married three times, a niggardly risk taker. Abram, Max, Aaron, Sasha—they all immersed themselves in earthly pleasures, in flight from boredom. They craved change, risk, danger. Obsession became their reality.

Almost every member of the tribe of Singer's males was passionate and, like Byron, lusted after women. One woman was not enough for any of them; none was calmed by a single woman. They could have written books about what went on on the sofas in their rooms. They cataloged innumerable quantities of breasts—large, firm, prominent, with fiery red nipples—and knees that promised all the pleasures of this world. They counted up kisses and traces of love bites. They praised earthly delights and even the delights of Turkish heavens, simultaneously with five or six lovers. Each of them knew it was a mortal sin, but the evil spirit played the role of master very well.

He gave his male protagonists his own anxieties. Like him, they were insatiable. Just like him, they "lust[ed] after the whole female gender." They were like a needle attracted to a powerful magnet. And all of them had a hysterical fear of impotence. They knew of no affliction with more power to unmask them.

"Why is there so much sex in your work?" people never tired of asking him.

"Dostoevsky was asked if every Russian is a murderer," he replied evasively. "Of course life is not made up of sex alone, but I like to write about sex just as Dostoevsky liked to write about murder. I see no reason why I shouldn't do that. And if you ask me does that help sales, yes, I admit that it does."

He wrote in his autobiography: "Those who rented rooms were nearly all women. . . . After a while they asked what I did and when I told them I worked for a publication they were instantly won over. Our glances met and mutely asked: perhaps? I had become a connoisseur of faces, bosoms, shoulders, bellies, hips. I speculated how much pleasure these various parts could provide if it came to an intimacy."

In public he was embarrassed by nudity.

He tried to kiss a journalist from the New York weekly *Village*

Voice while she was interviewing him. She didn't let him. As she was leaving, he asked, "And did you kiss *Borges?*"

He told her the story of how a man came to see his father, the rabbi, and announced that he wanted to marry a prostitute. "Why," Rabbi Singer wondered, "would you want to marry a prostitute who has had hundreds of men?" The man answered: "It's the way she spreads her legs; I have never met a woman who did it that way. I can't imagine life without her."

These are the confessions of a seventy-year-old man.

He was a writer of passions. The trap of lust and insatiability. The hunger for life. And voraciousness. He was not a writer of love.

Yet love existed in his world. If it didn't, then why did Magda hang herself when she was betrayed yet again by Yasha (*The Magician of Lublin*)? Why did Hadassah run away from her husband, or Clara (*The Family Moskat*)? How explain the behavior of Jadwiga, who risked her life by hiding Herman in her barn during all the years of the war (*Enemies, a Love Story*)? What caused Wanda to change into silent Sara if not her love for Jacob, a Jew, a man whom her faith forbade her to marry (*The Slave*)?

It's usually the women who love. The men only allow themselves to be loved. Or rather, their love doesn't cost much. They pay only with pangs of conscience. They sacrifice nothing, and they lose nothing. Their lives, in almost all of Singer's pairings, do not change because of love. Their lives are not turned upside down because those emotions and unions rarely demand exclusivity. They are capable of being calculating. Does Aaron Greidinger not love Shosha? He loves her. But at the same time he lives with Betty, Dora, and Celia.

Does Herman Broder not love Masha? He loves her. But he supplements her with Jadwiga and Tamara. Did Yasha not love Esther, Magda, Zeftel, and Emilia? He loved them all. He wanted to have them all and keep them all. It was they who fought for love. He just yielded to it. Until the moment when it began to bore him. Sated, he looked around for something new.

For Singer's heroes, love is more often a game than the fulfillment of an inner need for closeness, tenderness, sharing. It is a sort of hypnosis. They call it a chronic illness.

"Again, he felt love for her," he writes about Yasha. "He desired her body." That equation is repeated too frequently to be considered merely accidental. It is not, however, an expression, a proof, or even a sign of love. Singer insists that faithfulness isn't either.

The love of Jacob the slave for the peasant Wanda also began with lust. She gave up everything for him: her faith, her family, her past. Her name too. He, by yielding to their mutual passion, became the cause of her death. A quarter century later he returned to Pilica from the Holy Land in order to find her grave. The heroes of an impossible love were buried together.

He wrote *The Slave* in 1961, between *The Magician of Lublin* and *Enemies*. He was fifty-seven years old. Neither before nor after that did he tell a similar love story. This Jewish version of *Romeo and Juliet* contradicts his philosophy and, in a perverse way, confirms it. As an exception to the rule.

He was not a writer of love. Perhaps he was incapable of simplifying it? But he certainly was familiar with its yearnings.

His women are dead. Gina died. So did Clara, Hadassah,

Wanda. Magda and Masha took their own lives. Little Shosha did not survive the exodus from bombed-out Warsaw. "I will never leave you," Aaron, the author's alter ego, said to her. He kept his promise in his own way. Not only to her but to all of them.

ISRAEL, 1991   Mordechai Canin, born and raised in Poland, is a writer and the longtime president of the Association of Jewish Writers in Israel:

"Bashevis is not the greatest Jewish writer; there were better ones. His brother Joshua was definitely better than he was. Others—Asch, Bergelson—are no longer living; it's not easy to speak about myself, but people say I am a very good prose writer. My epic about the Wandering Jew is the first work of its kind in Jewish literature. A great Jewish poet said that he had considered writing something like that, but he couldn't manage it. But Singer was entrepreneurial, much more so than I am. If he weren't a Jew, he would probably have been an anti-Semite. Anyone who knows his prose in Yiddish, in the original, knows that he invents horrible things about Jews. But translations of Singer, in accord with his wishes, are not made from Yiddish, from the original. He works on them himself, discarding what needs to be discarded, and prepares translations into English. And he has a superb command of English. In addition, there are competent, energetic people in the editorial offices and publishing houses; they had an in with the academy, and he got the Nobel.

"Bashevis wrote a little before the war, for the Jewish press in Poland—cheap novels, trashy romances. Every day he would develop the plot to a dramatic point, for example, when he throws her onto the couch . . . to be continued. And that's how he became very popular; he saw that it sold. The main point is, he is obsessed with sex. It's fascinating how that happened to him. He comes from a rabbinical family; his father was the rabbi of Krochmalna Street. And there Singer came into contact with Jewish prostitutes, with thieves. Bashevis soaked it all up.

"He came to America in 1935. His brother worked at the *Forward*. Abraham Cahan was the editor of the paper at that time. He's dead; he would be one hundred thirty years old now. As long as Cahan was alive, they published Bashevis very reluctantly. No, not because of his eroticism; eroticism is good, but depravity is not. He is a cynic above all, a very smart, very witty cynic. And he laughs at his readers. He doesn't respect them. But he knows how to give them what they are looking for.

"Obviously, in order to give a certain class of readers what they want, all the filth in the world, including politics, could be found there. Singer gives what the masses want; more to the point, what the non-Jewish masses want too. They are especially good at picking up on certain anti-Semitic elements in his writing. There are very negative things about Jews there. He gave the goyim what they wanted, especially such an image of Jews. For example, I read the same text in English that I read in Yiddish. And it is something entirely different. It's clear that the English text is better.

"Please remember that the majority of Jewish immigrants in America were uneducated. The admirers of Singer, who swallowed those trashy stories, all those improbable absurdities, gutter-press pieces, sensational tales, were uneducated too. This is degenerate literature. The reader in America, the reader who reads Yiddish, came from a little town in Russia or Poland; that's the same audience he wrote for in the old country.

"The next editor of the *Forward* after Cahan was Hillel Rogow. At that time, in the fifties, Singer began writing and publishing more. It was on such an embarrassing level that it was completely unreadable. I'll tell you one scene, miss. A woman betrays her husband; suddenly the doorbell rings. The lover crawls under the bed; the husband enters. He talks with his wife. And what does the lover under the bed do in the meantime? He makes a hole in the mattress and copulates with the woman. Amusing? In the English version this scene is missing. He had that much intuition and common sense. Or, for example, he puts three women and two men into a bed—abnormal things like that. And a reader of a certain age lives in this false world; he is already old, but he wants to read such things. And Bashevis provided it for him. I have to grant him one thing. He is a magnificent storyteller; he knows how to sell those goods. His language is good; he has excellent Yiddish. And he is lucky. That is all that is necessary. But how much that man suffered before he achieved that success. I know that he was dying of hunger in America, because Cahan was a hard man and although he liked Singer's brother, he did not want to publish Bashevis.

"Singer is toilet pornography. That's what I would call it in Yiddish. Depraved literature but beautifully narrated. It's dangerous, a divine talent. If it's a question of its worth, I don't value it highly. But once you begin reading, you can't stop."

⫴ THEY CALLED HIM A PORNOGRAPHER ⫴

NEW YORK, 1992   Abraham Shulman attended the Spójnia Gymnasium at No. 27 Długa Street in Warsaw. One day in the 1920s he stood up in Polish class and said, "Professor, I have an idea: They should take down the monument to Adam Mickiewicz and put up mine."

"We'll think about it," replied his teacher.

"I met Bashevis for the first time in the *Forward*'s editorial room in the forties. I had come to New York from Paris, where I was the paper's correspondent. When they brought me upstairs to meet my colleagues, I noticed an unprepossessing little man in the corner with blue, almost transparent eyes. I asked who that was. Bashevis. *The* Bashevis? I went over to him immediately (I knew his writings) and said, 'It's a great joy to meet you in person.'

" 'What kind of joy?' he replied. 'When you know the cook, you can't like his cooking.'

"That day he had nothing left to do, so we went out together into the street. The Lower East Side reminded one of the old country in those days. It was crowded and noisy. Men with *peyess,* women wearing wigs, street vendors of slippers and underwear. The smell of marinated herring, sauerkraut, and pickles. Signs: tallithim and mezuzahs. He didn't say much; he was in a melancholy mood.

" 'What are you writing now?' I asked.

" 'Oh, I'm scribbling something or other,' he answered.

"In the beginning he was terribly sad, beaten down; he told me that twice after his arrival in America he'd wanted to commit suicide. The conditions in that newspaper office were terrible. I saw how they treated him. At that time I was the only reviewer who had positive things to say about him. Because of that, I experienced a good deal of unpleasantness; writers practically didn't speak to me. I received anonymous letters from readers. One was even written in the form of a sonnet. The author wished me all the worst, that I should break my arms and legs and not have the strength to write such ravings.

"And when I began traveling around America on lecture tours, I was always warned: 'Think about it; it will be a disaster if you talk about Bashevis. Talk about Peretz, Sholem Aleichem, about anyone you want, but not about him.' I didn't listen to them. Sometimes people even came to blows. I remember once in Miami a woman left the auditorium, screaming, 'I am not going to listen to talk about Goebbels!'

"People said he was a pornographer. The Jewish critics accused him of anti-Semitism, of depicting Jews as sinners, fornicators, worthless individuals, vile creatures. They believed that after what had happened during the war, it was forbidden to write about Jews in that way. Some critics called him a pogromist, a Bohdan Chmielnicki.

"I used to go to his talks; sometimes he came to mine. I remember the archbishop's words after his appearance in a church in Boston: 'Up until now I did not know the Jewish people, but now, reading Bashevis, I have come to know and love them.' This happened at the same time that Jews were saying his writing was offensive and false.

"That evening in the church, in the middle of giving his lecture he suddenly read a story in Yiddish. It was unbelievable, but the Catholic, English-speaking audience listened in absolute silence. When he finished, they applauded. I asked him afterward what was the point of reading in Yiddish since no one understood a single word. 'How do you know,' he responded, 'that not understanding is not the highest degree of understanding?'

"He was a very sad man. Nothing made him happy.

"Before he left for America, he lived in Warsaw. His older brother was a painter and a writer, a talented writer; some people consider him better than Bashevis. Isaac was red-haired, wore Hasidic *peyess*. He had a mistress in Warsaw, a Communist. She became pregnant and told him, 'Come, let's smuggle ourselves across the border to Moscow.' But he didn't want to. So she left on her own, with their son. In the end they wound up in Palestine. When I got to know Bashevis, I said, 'They have invited you to Israel now; you are publishing more pieces all the time. Go, you'll see your son.'

" 'I can't; I'd have to buy him a present.' That's what he said. When the son finally came here, they saw each other in dairy bars, coffee shops. And now he translates his father from English into Hebrew. He also spoke at the funeral. In English.

"It wasn't a Jewish funeral at all. He, who had spoken Yiddish to the king of Sweden in Stockholm, did not hear a single Yiddish word at his own funeral. A rabbi with a black beard from the nearby synagogue gave a talk. He said he asked Bashevis once, 'What is the mission of literature?'

" 'If I had a mission, I would have been a rabbi,' he answered.

"For him, literature was telling a story.

"He was boring. True, in company, during meetings with the public, he spoke wittily, even brilliantly; he wrote like that too. But he was a very uninteresting person in daily life. The critics were always comparing him to Homer, Cervantes, even Kierkegaard. There was always someone like that in the little Jewish towns who came and told stories. Bashevis was actually someone like that.

"He was incapable of taking care of anything, and left to himself, he would not have won the Nobel. That kind of character. But other people realized, after Saul Bellow published his translation of 'Gimpel the Fool,' that they could make money on him. They started coming to him and taking; he didn't even know what; he was the last to know about the films made from his works.

"He wasn't liked. At his funeral there was no one from the newspaper offices where he'd worked for so many years. They hated him.

"Why? I'll tell you a story. He was asked once on television if Yiddish literature is good. He answered: 'Very good.'

" 'Great?'

" 'Very great.'

" 'Does it have many great poets and writers?'

" 'Yes, many.'

" 'Please name some.'

" 'Oh, you're asking me to remember, and my memory is nonfunctional.'

"He didn't say anything about anyone. Not a word.

"A terrible skinflint, a terrible womanizer. I give you my word on both counts.

"I myself met him with several women. For example, with a beautiful young woman who was a German Jew. She said she was a follower of Spinoza. She asked me to introduce her to him. (After his lectures there was always a line of girls, and I would give them his telephone number.) On the next day she called and asked me to give Bashevis a letter from her. I said that I would give him the letter under one condition: I had to read it. 'You have Oriental manners if you read other people's letters.' She bristled, but she opened the letter. Enclosed was a color photograph of her, entirely naked. 'Call me, call me, call me . . . ' and a telephone number. Afterward he described it all in the Yiddish newspaper.

"He had success with women, he did, he certainly did. At one exhibition opening Bashevis arrived with a very young girl. He said, 'She's a Catholic from Oklahoma; she read my books, went to a rabbi, converted to Judaism, and came here to meet me in person.' I also used to think that he was just telling tall tales. But *that* he didn't invent. He invented other things, but not that.

"What did his wife think about that? She knew about everything. She is a German Jew. God forbid that you should go to visit her and sit with her even for five hours, you won't get a glass of tea. Once after five hours I got a glass of water. He was a great writer but a petty man. A strange man. He didn't want to see his son because he'd have to buy a present.

"Where did that come from? Maybe from his memories of poverty?

"I hate Freud, and I am opposed to psychology, but his miserliness was so sick that it could not have been only a problem from his past.

"We were very close friends, and then throughout 1972 we wrote a play together based on his story 'Taybele and Her Demon.' When we had finished the first act, he said, 'I am going to take you to lunch tomorrow; I'll pay; don't eat anything today, you'll eat your fill tomorrow.'

"Naturally I went home and stuffed myself with two dinners. Across Eighty-sixth Street there used to be a cafeteria; he wrote about it a lot. We went there. The waiter came over; he had on an apron on which you could see the entire menu. He said, 'Take what I tell you.'

"I agreed. It was several, literally several, green peas. He chose yogurt for himself. I ate quickly because I thought it was an appetizer, but he said, 'Coffee we'll have in my house.'

"How can you be angry at such a man? You can't.

"I have an acquaintance who's a typist, and I wanted to give her the play to type up, the play that Bashevis and I had written together. 'For him,' she said, 'I'm not going to type; he won't pay.'

" 'How can that be?' I said. 'Look at how much he pub-lishes.'

" 'But he spends all his money on the pigeons in the park,' she replied.

"That's what he'd told her: that he spends everything on birds.

"Apropos of women. I know one young Jewish woman, a jour-nalist from Zurich, in Switzerland. Her editor assigned her to write an essay on Singer. Bashevis was already sick with Alz-heimer's, there couldn't be any connection, but she didn't know that. She got on an airplane and flew straight to Miami. She arrived at Singer's house without any warning. She said, 'I am from Switzerland, I came to have an interview with Mr. Bash-evis Singer.' She was so preoccupied with her mission that she didn't notice how much she'd upset his wife. After a while she noticed a motionless figure in an armchair next to the window, like a mannequin. It was Singer. She understood. She began to wriggle out of it. 'I should have written, should have notified you,' she explained.

"Suddenly, he had a flash of consciousness; he turned his head, 'An interview? . . . Ask.'

"She said, 'No . . . no. . . . '

" 'Ask.'

" 'Very well,' she said, 'just one question: What is the greatest pleasure in life?'

"Then he lifted his arms, moving them apart in an ex-aggerated gesture of helplessness, and replied quite clearly, 'A girl . . . '

"And she wrote it down. Apparently that was the last conscious word he said in his life."

FLORIDA, 1992   K. worked as a correspondent for the War-saw Yiddish daily *Moment*; he also published a Yiddish weekly in Płock. His brother was the last secretary-general of the Union of Jewish Writers and Journalists at No. 13 Tłomackie. When K. came to Warsaw, he used his brother's card to get into the theaters.

In America he worked in the editorial offices of the *Forward* for twenty-five years as a proofreader.

"Bashevis was a regular associate of our newspaper. He con-tributed two articles weekly. They usually ran on Fridays and Saturdays. He never trusted anyone; he always had to come himself and check to see if we had let any mistakes slip through. It would create a lot of confusion because he usually came in at the last minute, when the issue was already locked in and ready to be sent to the printer. We begged him to show up early so the paper could come out on time. It never helped. In the old days we used to work on linotype machines; changing the typesetting was even more complicated then than now. But he would stand over you and watch to see that everything was done right.

"He never came to the editorial offices just to talk or to gossip. Occasionally he would drop into the coffee shop on

Broadway where the artists and writers sat around. In general he was a very likable man, but every now and then he could stick a pin into someone.

"I talked with him on many occasions. In Yiddish, only in Yiddish. 'Mr. Bashevis, don't worry, go home, there won't be any mistakes. You can trust us.' But he always said, 'Oh, no, no, no, I have to read it myself. I have to see for myself how it is.' He read out loud; he mumbled and nodded his head over the text. He came, he read, he read, he left, and that was that.

"He wrote his articles longhand. He was very accurate; he checked all his quotations himself. Other people did that sloppily. He was meticulous, smart; he could answer right off the bat like no one else could. His manuscripts were legible. We chose intelligent linotypists who knew his style to set his articles. Sometimes it happened that a typesetter would correct something. Of course that would be checked with him before printing, and if he thought it was a good change, he was pleased.

"His clothes weren't especially elegant; they were actually quite ordinary. Even later, when he was working steadily at the *Forward* and had a good income. He received the highest honoraria. Just about everything he wrote was first printed in installments in our newspaper. He stopped working for us only when the daily *Forward* became a weekly. He resigned over money. He had begun to demand sky-high payments for his articles. The *Forward* couldn't pay that much. That was in the eighties, after the death of Weber, the editor. Yes, after the Nobel. He was criticized for that because after all, the *Forward* was his place; that's where his career got started, and he achieved popularity thanks to that paper. But he had a peculiar attitude toward money. 'I'd like to give you a larger tip,' he once told a waiter in a restaurant, 'but my heart won't let me.'

" 'He's not human,' people said about him. When he came to New York, various people helped him out, not just writers. He was poor; he didn't have what to live on. But he never helped anyone afterward. If someone came to him and asked for something, he'd answer sympathetically, but as for doing something, nothing of the sort. It was impossible to come to him and ask for help, especially, God forbid, for money.

"He wanted to be popular, like everyone. He gave lectures. When it was question time, he answered wittily, rapidly. He was eccentric, exceptionally self-centered. But how he wrote! It's alive; you can see those types in front of you.

"He wasn't at all involved with politics. He had nothing to do with the Polish language. It didn't interest him at all, just as traveling back to Poland didn't. He was an opponent of communism, he wrote about that. Runia, his first wife, was a Communist.

"A Don Juan? I don't know. In my opinion, he wrote and talked about it more than it actually happened in reality. He made a lot of noise. But he wasn't that appealing; he wasn't attractive. He was sort of sneaky.

"Sometimes we would talk about it among ourselves: Look at that, he's describing such things with women; today he slept with one woman, yesterday with another. We didn't believe it. No, we didn't ask him; he wouldn't have answered. We thought it was fantasy."

⦚ Filth ⦚

"I didn't know Singer personally, but I think that he did not deserve the Nobel Prize. For many reasons. I'll even say this: During his lifetime he was not considered a great Jewish writer. It was his brother who was a great Jewish writer.

"In his stories he often referred to his brother: 'My brother guided me,' 'My brother taught me.' And that's the truth. Why do I speak of him bitingly? I'll tell you; maybe you'll understand. Why was he received the way he was and why was he translated as he was? Because of his subject matter, because of his characterization of Jews, those small-town Jews, as sexually sick people with diabolical ideas, fantasizing, dreaming, always talking about things that are rarely encountered in human experience. And he did this at a time when those same women, that same society had been sent to the gas—then and afterward. He became a great writer by writing that . . . filth. Filth!

"There are other Jewish writers who deserve awards and recognition. You too were misled by Singer, the Nobel Prize winner. That's one side of the coin. But I am going to tell you about the other side. A painter of Jewish society! But that society also was based on something else! Did he, for example, ever write about the Jews' contribution to Polish economic life? To the construction of that life? Did he write about university professors, about the contributions of Jews to Polish medicine? Never. He wrote about tradesmen, thieves, prostitutes; that's not the image of Jewish life in other writers. In Chaim Grade, for example. And what is in Grade? Everything that characterizes all people who live in one place for a long time. The life of ordinary people, their stories, sayings. Grade was from Vilnius. It wasn't Singer who deserved that prize. He didn't get it for his greatness as a writer, but for his subject matter. I wouldn't even call it a slice of life. You cannot judge the Jewish people on the basis of his stories. You can't. And you shouldn't.

"I'll give you an example that defines the man. His name was Singer, but he signed himself Bashevis in order to distinguish himself from his brother. Every week he wrote his little stories for the *Forward*. At that time there was a major discussion among Jews about the future of Yiddish, and during the war, in the flood of horrifying news about what was happening in Poland, this too was discussed in his paper. And that man, sometimes under the name Bashevis and sometimes as Singer, wrote entirely contradictory things. One of them said that Yiddish has no future; the other, that it does. The same man. At the same time. For me that's enough. You can interpret it as you like. I give you the fact, and you interpret it. I give you an example of authorial morality.

"I used to work for the Yiddish paper *Haynt* in Poland, during the twenty-year period from Poland's independence until the occupation of Warsaw. I had no contact with him in Warsaw. He was Singer's younger brother, insignificant.

"When I wrote my book, the history of the newspaper, I wanted to know something more about him; someone told me that he had a sister who also wrote. I sent him a letter asking him for information, so I could include it. He didn't respond. That little fact is disgusting.

"A great man, a Nobel laureate . . . I am definitely not a great man, but neither is he. In my opinion, awarding him the Nobel Prize was an offense to Jews. Rumor has it that some university professor who read *The New Yorker* and became acquainted with Singer's work through it was the one who nominated him. He was the only Jewish writer that man was aware of. And since Europe is unable to free itself of its feeling of guilt, is unable to live with the knowledge that they did nothing to prevent the extermination of the entire Jewish people, they wanted to finally make some kind of a gesture. Perhaps 'gesture' is the wrong word; they wanted to redeem themselves by supporting a language that had died together with an entire people. Maybe that was the motivation of the Nobel committee. How much truth there is in this idea, I don't know. But it's what people say.

"My father was a teacher in a Russian-language public school. From 1909 to 1914. He made me study Polish; it wasn't required. My parents spoke Yiddish with each other, Polish with us children. And we children spoke Yiddish among ourselves. When Papa died, I was seventeen. He left his widow and six children. I was the oldest. Before the war I worked for one year for a Zionist organization and a Zionist newspaper. The staff of that paper went over to *Haynt*. I did too, as a reporter. I wrote, I read, and I observed. In Warsaw there were five important Jewish dailies. Ours was the most oppositional in relation to the government.

"I was always a Jew; I was never a Pole. The Poles didn't consider a single Jew to be a Pole, not the most assimilated. Not even those who rode in carriages to the Tłomackie Synagogue on Yom Kippur—they too were thought of as Jews. Even though they considered themselves the greatest of Poles.

"I am a Jew, and I am thought of as a Jew. At every step. Here they think they're Americans. You ask me when I first felt that I am a Jew. And when did I first feel myself breathe? It was natural. I was a Pole here, in America. For a long time I carried a Polish passport. I didn't want to give it up; I thought it would be a betrayal. But no one considered me a Pole, not over there and not here.

"Singer published those loathsome stories. He made a career writing what he wrote when the victims were already incinerated. There was nothing else for him to write about? A people had perished, their life, their culture, and he chose sordidness, presenting it as the life of the people. The Jewish people has a right to their sordidness, but think how many Jews have won awards for science, for medicine, for physics. That, he didn't write about. Life is not made up only of roses. But to write about sordidness on the ashes of his father and mother and God knows who else! That disgusts me; it disgusted me in the past, and it will always disgust me."

⅓| A PAPER BRIDGE |Ƚ

NEW YORK, 1993   Legend says that when the Messiah comes, the Jews will cross over to the Land of Israel on a paper bridge.

Everything that he wrote was such a bridge across the ocean to the old country. A bridge that connected him with his source. With a planet that was a paradise lost, a hell, and a nonexistent promised land.

A bridge is a link between what has been disconnected in time and in space. A link between two worlds, the seen and the unseen, God and man. A safe transition to a state of initiation.

Someone once said that he looked like a worker in a matzoh factory who had never been exposed to sunlight. People joked that he was the palest man on the Upper West Side, the district of Manhattan where he lived. A balding man, his remaining hair gray, with a birdlike head, a hooked nose, no eyebrows, and very penetrating blue eyes. He was frequently seen taking a walk along Broadway or feeding the pigeons in Central Park. A short, thin figure in a dark suit and hat, moving with unhurried, ever-slower steps.

He liked this part of the city with its atmosphere that reminded him of prewar Warsaw, with the tastes and smells of childhood, the shadows of the past. He liked the small dairy bars and cafeterias, where food was cheap and familiar, and the waiters didn't urge people to leave. He would take a seat there in order to eat something and to converse in Yiddish with people like himself, Jewish refugees from Eastern Europe. He liked the street itself, with its sounds and traffic, continually astonished once again by the wealth of human types. Thinking up new and different variants for his heroes' fates. Always in search of life stories.

He wrote at a round table, in the corner between two windows, facing Broadway, in a ponderous Secession-style building, which he chose because its large courtyard reminded him of Warsaw courtyards. He wrote in a dying language about a nonexistent world, condemning himself to a double isolation. The soil from which he drew his literary juices had dried up. He replaced it with recollections.

"My past is my future," he said repeatedly.

Yiddish literature became a memory book.

Before the war a Jewish writer in Poland could go out into the street and "fill himself with the voices" of Jewish life in all its colorful variety. Daily life "kept an eye on literature"; "ritual maintained control over it." Forms existed without which it is difficult for great art to exist, patterns that lent themselves to "rewriting." Simply put, it was living reality.

In America the Yiddish language had become over time in-authentic in relation to the life that developed there. It was a language from somewhere else, a language of the past. It seems as if Singer was able to describe only what he knew intimately. But now everything had passed on into the indefinite space of memory. He rarely ventured beyond it. He never allowed himself to be evicted from there or from the language that shaped his remembering.

His muse remained little Shosha, the Beatrice of the street of Jewish poverty. She personified the world of ancient tradition, so different from the contemporary world, whose moral categories struck him as suspect. In her dedication to her faith, God, and one man, Shosha was naive, perhaps provincial and anachronistic, perhaps not rising to the intellectual and emotional ambitions of modernity. He seemed to be just like that himself. With his absurdly stubborn insistence on remaining in the charmed circle of Jewishness, which had succumbed to annihilation. With his marriage to illiterate Shosha.

He was tempted to abandon her. Like Yasha, the Magician of Lublin, who was led astray in the end by the possibility of entering the worldly reality of his Polish mistress. But flight from himself and his God proved impossible. His reaching out for something foreign was punished. Singer seems to be warning himself here: Abandoning one's tradition, denying one's spiritual belonging, carries with it crippling deformity and emptiness. Immersion in American culture borders on self-annihilation. Erasure of the traces of identity would have been a disaster.

Yasha's truth is Singer's truth: Perhaps in confinement there is a path to a broader perspective, in imprisonment the one true freedom?

He lived on Manhattan's Upper West Side for thirty years, almost as long as in Poland. In a neighborhood of Jewish intellectuals and students, not far from Columbia University and Symphony Space, a literary theater. Near the Hudson River, on Broadway, where he could meet the living and the dead. A heroine in one of his stories stumbled across a meeting of the Nazi party, where she saw Hitler. That same night the building in which this took place burned. The suicides strolled arm in arm with their wealthy relatives, and beggars sang songs full of hope.

New York fascinated him. The intensity of the life flowing on in that city, daily, every moment; it was enough simply to go outside. At the same time he considered it the most private city on earth. It was easy to preserve one's anonymity there. That too he valued.

In America they mostly read English-language books. Translations from obscure languages seldom make it onto the bestseller lists. The English-language version of *The Family Moskat*, published by Knopf in 1950, took five years to translate and was not a commercial success. It seemed likely that Singer was destined to live his life at the *Forward*, with his Yiddish readers as his audience. But in 1953 Saul Bellow, already a well-known writer, translated "Gimpel the Fool," and the story became an instant literary sensation. The New York critic Irving Howe called Singer a genius, and his stories began to appear regularly in important American magazines, from the *Saturday Evening Post* to *Playboy*.

Roger Straus, one of the doyens of American publishing, threw his firm's weight behind Singer, bringing out a number of his books. Awards and distinctions followed. In 1970 Singer received the National Book Award for a volume of his memoirs. Four years later he was honored with the same prize, this time for fiction.

On October 5, 1978, in Miami Beach, where the Singers had resided since 1973, Isaac received the news that he was awarded the Nobel Prize in Literature, the highest honor available to a writer. The phone call came in the morning. "Let's have some breakfast," he said to Alma after hanging up the phone. "There's no reason not to eat because of some award."

In Stockholm he spoke of writing in a dying language. It is a language beloved by ghosts, he said, and who are the heroes of his stories if not ghosts themselves?

In America there had been no war, yet New York is not the same city it was years ago.

Even the Lower East Side, where Jewish immigrants had once rediscovered their past, speaks for the most part in Spanish with a Puerto Rican accent. The children of the tailors and street vendors, survivors of successive holocausts, are successful lawyers and doctors and seek out safer places to live, in New Jersey, Connecticut, or Long Island. But the pulse of immigration continues to beat, although today they come from Tula and Yerevan rather than Biłgoraj. The next Singer, if one should be born, will remember Odessa.

Only his wife, Alma, still returns home as he used to, slowly, laboriously, as if Broadway were a summit to be conquered. It is evening, and no one is waiting for her. Perhaps that is why she is fearless.

In Au Petit Beurre one can sit for hours over one cup of coffee and look out at Broadway. I met people there who belonged to his world: several who knew him from before the war and many whom he might have described. A boy who survived the war in the uniform of the Hitlerjugend and came to our meeting with his old photograph. A man who was ordered to choose between his own mother's death and the death of the mother of his children. A woman who still does not know who she is. (She hasn't cut her braids. She couldn't. How else would her father recognize her after fifty years?) Another woman who was a German officer's mistress and saved someone's family. They ended their lives many times and began anew.

To learn what it was like before the war, it's best to read Singer. Not many people are able to explain beyond what someone condensed into two sentences: that they were young and beautiful. Therefore the world—despite everything—seemed young and beautiful too. "Now we are old and deaf and we have trouble getting about." And the world of their memories, after all, is not rosy.

The war is the most important boundary. That was when they learned how quickly one can lose everything. They are always prepared now. They don't form attachments to anything.

He wrote a few stories about the lives of Jews in America. But it took him over a quarter of a century to decide to do that. And he still was not certain if he really knew anything.

In the dairy bar on Seventy-second Street where he was a regular guest, he usually sat at the same table in the back of the dining area, not far from the old box that houses the air conditioner. Sam Orenstein, a waiter who never read any of his books, says he was an ordinary man. "He didn't demand much. It just turned out that he became a hero."

He had certain habits that he always adhered to. He didn't pay for anyone, and he didn't want anyone to pay for him. "What do we have for lunch today, Semkele?" he invariably asked. He usually took the special for $5.50: mushroom or barley soup and vegetarian chopped liver on rye. Plus dessert—rice pudding, cheese cake, or stewed prunes—and coffee. Roger Straus, an aristocrat among New York publishers, remembers with a tolerant smile that Singer used to drag him to cheap eateries where he would order him to eat vegetarian hamburgers.

I found many places like that. In the somewhat better ones the dishes looked less greasy, and jars of pickles and sauerkraut were on the tables. People would be speaking in Yiddish or heavily accented English (it was said of Singer that he spoke Yiddish in every language). More often they spoke in Russian, particularly in the Brooklyn neighborhood called Little Odessa. Not far from there are the streets that Singer knew from his early years in America. And that his heroes knew too.

Like Herman from *Enemies*, he liked to walk Brooklyn's streets, which reminded him of streets in Poland. On Mermaid Avenue Yiddish advertisements for rabbis and cantors were posted on the walls of buildings right next to price lists for seats in the synagogue on Yom Kippur. "The smells of chicken soup, kasha, and chopped liver emanated from restaurants and coffee houses. The bakeries were selling bagels, egg twists, and onion rolls. In front of the stores women were blindly digging in pickle barrels."

He could never believe that there is a place on this earth where Jews can live in peace. He settled into this daily existence with its familiar forms, but at the same time he could not forget what had happened. He thought about where and how he would manage to hide.

Isaac Bashevis writes that "it was not given to him to experience the Holocaust." His twin hero chooses a different fate. Asa Heshel from *The Family Moskat* decides to remain in besieged Warsaw in full consciousness of the imminent destruction of the city and its Jews. He does not want to survive. He wants to die.

Similarly, Aaron Greidinger from *Shosha*, despite an invitation to travel to America, does not leave Poland. Instead of running away, he marries Shosha, his childhood friend, demonstrating by this gesture, which many people consider mad, his faithfulness to his Jewish world on the eve of catastrophe.

He did not allow his heroes who survived to forget.

They were unable to tell "the whole truth" about their wartime fates. They awoke screaming in the middle of the night. Persecuted, hunted, beaten. "Has anyone ever died of nightmares?" Masha wondered in *Enemies*. And with pointed mockery looked around the lake outside New York and asked, "Where are the Nazis? What kind of world is it without fascists? It's a backward country, this America."

Herman's closeness to Masha gave him the opportunity to experience what had been spared him in his hiding place in the barn. He wanted to experience her humiliation and fear in order to free himself from the guilty feelings that never left him. He felt compelled to justify fate's having been kinder to him than to others. Was this a problem for the author of *Enemies* too?

So many people still walk down the nonexistent streets of nonexistent cities today, cutting their way through labyrinths of memory.

These few who survived have reconstructed internal landscapes. They have assimilated alien places well enough to be able to live in them. But there are always fragments of a former reality. Old, transplanted trees.

I attempted to enter that world. I disturbed people's memories and the earth itself in search of the traces. In Poland I groped my way through the remnants of an old landscape. Fragments of walls, shadows of streets, people. It only seemed easier in America. On New York's Lower East Side, in Brooklyn, in Florida.

I was seeking something I had never known: imagined tastes and smells. Singer was a master at describing them and that helped me. But I was always intruding from outside.

"You are a tourist in this world," someone said to me.

"And you?" I asked.

"I? I live here."

Bashevis went to Florida for the first time in the winter of 1948. It seemed to him that his past had found him there. The cafeterias in Miami reminded him of the Jewish Writers' Club in Warsaw. People dropped in there every day to discuss politics or literature or just to gossip. He felt a similar mood even some fifteen years after the war. Later there were fewer and fewer places like that; more elegant restaurants sprang up. "The spirit of the old world had disappeared."

When he came to America, he was homesick for the old country. He founds traces of it in Miami in the forties and fifties. Then he was homesick for the old Miami.

Flaubert said that never having seen them, one finds it easier to imagine deserts, pyramids, and sphinxes than "the face of a Turkish barber sitting cross-legged in front of his doorstep." Singer held a similar opinion. That is why his gallery of portraits and character types is so rich. That is why he described eyes, noses, chins, signs, and humpbacks in such detail.

I was still able to see those faces. Aged, weary, and full of wrinkles. How do they differ from other faces? By a particular expression in the eyes, in which sadness is mixed with the conviction that everything that happened and is yet to happen is necessary?

I meet a Jewish girl from Biłgoraj, most likely Isaac Bashevis Singer's last surviving contemporary, in Miami Beach. The old woman repeats triumphantly: "I remember him, I remember."

"Please tell me what you remember," I encourage her.

She freezes, withdraws into that world to which I have no access. Perhaps she is in the market square on market day, seeing the birds in their nests near the new synagogue, gathering acorns under the oaks in the Jewish cemetery. I don't know where she is.

"I remember, I remember . . ." she repeats. "He was such a redhead, such a redhead. . . ."

Nothing more.

They come to Miami Beach to get some rest. They come to Miami Beach to die. They escape from the New York winters to rest under the palm trees and the bright southern sun. People refer to Miami Beach, MB, as *miasteczko Bełz*, the *Bełz shtetl*, but not everyone appreciates the comparison. When he used that term in an article, Singer was even called an anti-Semite; it wasn't the first or last time he was called that. Boardinghouses stretch out along the main street. Cheaper or more expensive, small, low buildings with furnished rooms for rent for the whole winter. On the ocean side there are elegant apartment houses and high-rise hotels with their own swimming pools and private beaches. The Jews from Lubartów and Zamość live there too.

They sit on beach chairs on the terraces, in the shade, under umbrellas. There are more women than men. They have hair in colors never found in nature, an excess of pink, and swimsuits that remind one of prewar cretonne beach costumes. Golden bracelets around their wrists; above them, their Auschwitz numbers. They smell of mothballs or Helena Rubinstein perfumes.

They have deeply concealed histories. Dressed with prewar elegance or bright American garishness, they stroll slowly along the boardwalk. They feed herds of neighborhood cats. The men play chess or cards. Sometimes they sing, accompanying themselves on the accordion. They pray, but without exaggeration. They don't like to touch their memories. They don't like to "remove" their smiles.

I move among them cautiously. They keep their old lives in inaccessible trunks of memory. Here they were born anew. Sometimes—in the sunshine, next to the ocean, in a swimming pool near one of the skyscrapers, during a walk in the sand— sometimes they begin to speak about Poland.

That when they were being deported from Firlej, the locals sang, "The Yids are being sent away."

That in Chełm the walls of the Catholic church were red with Jewish blood.

That in Izbica Polish firefighters pointed the way to Jewish hideouts.

That a Polish woman who saved them was forced to leave

her village because people came and threatened her, saying she should give up the valuables she'd received from the Jews. But she hadn't taken anything; she had done everything without demanding any compensation.

That after liberation Mother had gone to the peasants to reclaim the things she had given them for safekeeping, but she never came back; they killed her.

They remember that. How closely do their memories reflect reality?

How many of them have I spoken with by now? How many of them were moved at the sight of me, rediscovering in their incorrect Polish the taste of something that was lost forever? How many wept in front of me? Pulled out snapshots? How many accused me, blamed me for all the wrongs done to them by Poles? Virtually every day brings a new fate. A new discovery, a new element in this weaving.

Sometimes, when they hear me speak in Polish, they offer me a job. Housekeeping, cleaning. Because why else would a Pole come to a Jew abroad? Don't be offended. We now have very good relations. But this is the first time I've heard about somebody writing a book about this. . . . For whom?

"Those who have once stood on the threshold of death remain dead," someone tells me. And then I read the same thing in Singer. Not once; many times. They said about themselves, "We have no hope, and one dies more quickly from that than from cancer." And then they attempted to build everything anew.

———

They are seventy, eighty, ninety years old. Sometimes they dance at the weddings of grandsons and great-grandsons. They swim in the swimming pools. They buy new hats. And they sit in Miami Beach beside the ocean, asking why no one wept for them there in the old country.

Not far from the main promenade is a monument erected to the victims of the war: In the vault of the stone sky there is a single star, yellow, with the inscription "Jude."

⁋| The Final Letter |⁋

"It's terrible waiting so long," you wrote. Your mother told you that sinners in Gehenna lie on beds of nails and wait for letters.

But you never responded. I didn't think you would change your habits. Up there.

I visited the place where you were born. The orchard, in bloom then, is now filled with stunted fruit. No one knows anything. No one heard; no one remembers.

I visited the place where you died. In America. I went for a stroll along the avenue that carries your name. I spoke with people who drank coffee with you. I looked out the window at the ocean, the same window that you looked out of. The view is the same.

I visited the place where you lie buried. A Jewish cemetery in New Jersey that is almost half a century old. The pink granite monument is visible from a distance. Not many trees, a few shrubs around it. On the tablet, an inscription: "Creation was his joy." Do you remember Harry's hesitation over the inscription on Boris Lemkin's gravestone in your story? "Dear Boris, be healthy and happy wherever you are." Everyone tried to convince him that it is sacrilege to wish good health to a corpse. You thought differently.

Nearby a strong sunburned man is mowing the grass. He comes from Poland. From a small town in the south, not far from your father's hometown. These graves contain three times as many people as live in this man's hometown. How can one explain the presence of a *shabbos goy* at your grave?

According to the Bible, Jacob and Laban built a stone mound as a sign of the covenant. Jacob called it in Hebrew "pile of witness." Stones are signs of memory. Several stones have been placed on your grave, and two bouquets of already dried-out flowers lie beside them. Jews don't bring flowers to a cemetery.

"When one contemplates the sky the place where one is seems insignificant," you said. Is the sky really the same everywhere? In America and in Poland, with Jews and without Jews, in despair and in love?

"I am earth, I am the sun, I am the galaxy, I am a letter or a dot in the God's infinite book," you wrote. "Even if I am an error in God's work, I can't be completely erased. . . . God is the sum total not only of all deeds but also of all the possibilities. Good night, heaven. If you can, have mercy upon me."

DATE DUE

APR 2 2 2013			

GAYLORD · · · · · · · PRINTED IN U.S.A.